Advance Praise

Confession gets a bad rap in memoir—and taken in the modern context might deserve it. But here you have the confessions of Paul Zarzyski, ex-altar boy, defined in the truest sense of the word: as an exploration of our deepest motivations, an acknowledgment of what's sacred, an articulation of what we've come to understand and how we've come to know it. In this sense, confession stands as the true mark of an examined life. There are no slick sidesteps, no pulled punches in the whole of this book, and no apologies—just fifty poems and lyrics as exquisite and heartfelt as any I've read, and one memoir essay that draws you deep into the making of the man and the poet, this lover of fire and ice and 8-second rides. Equal parts exploration and celebration, music and message, Zarzyski's poems and prose come together like a long-married couple takes the dance floor for a midnight waltz.

Judy Blunt
Author of *Breaking Clean*

Paul Zarzyski writes with a pencil printed with bite marks, a "wood processor"—a Dixon Ticonderoga wood-cased black-core Number 2—not with the mega bits and toothless bytes of the word processor, an invention he disdains. This makes sense because his subject—carried out in unforgettable poetry and prose—is the timeless duel between love and death. Which, to paraphrase William Butler Yeats, is literature's only subject.

Rick DeMarinis
Author of *Mama's Boy*

From family to romance, from rodeo to politics, whether slantwise with humor or dead-on serious, Paul Zarzyski's cadences and imagery find a unique and powerful voice that always draws me right in. The bonus of a self-interview in this collection is truly engaging in the way it paints the writer's family, friends, and influences, and traces the blue-collar poetics that hold them all together in his poems and lyrics. With Zarzyski, the heart is always out there in front, showing its compassion for the *other* in race, gender and species—though the mind is always there, too, with its obvious complexity, its Whitman influences, and its instinctive knowledge of the American tradition.

Greg Keeler
Author of *Trash Fish*

Paul Zarzyski's *51* is language heightened to the elegant truths we sometimes miss or ignore: our commonality with all creatures requires communion, there are way too many missed connections, we ought to celebrate friendships and family more and mourn less, defiance is honorable in nearly every suspect circumstance, and generosity and valor are not too much to ask of ourselves. For those readers new to Paul Zarzyski, the poems and songs in *51* will go right to the heart. For Paul Zarzyski readers, those who have long appreciated his poetry, the self-interview is a treasure-trove of autobiography, anecdotes on the wild Missoula years of great writers having outlandish fun while getting the work done, hard-earned thoughts on poetry and songwriting, and matters of the spirit. Paul Zarzyski's *51* is a triumph in behalf of those with big hearts, because he is kin.

Red Shuttleworth
Author of *Western Settings*

1929 Corona Z-Buckle Sculpture: a Gift in Tribute to Paul's Poetry.

Vince Pedroia
Author of *A Mano*

51

3o Poems
2o Lyrics
1 Self-Interview

Paul Zarzyski

Bangtail
Press

Montana
2011

ISBN-13: 978-0-9828601-1-3

Manufactured in the United States of America

On page 165, "The Horseman, The Poet, The Code, The Horse," is from *All This Way for the Short Ride: Roughstock Sonnets 1971-1996*, courtesy Museum of New Mexico Press, Poems © 1996 Paul Zarzyski.

The poems, *The Hand, Montana Second Hand, Grace, Putting the Rodeo Try into Cowboy Poetry, Words Growing Wild in the Woods*, and *Face-to-Face*, first appeared in "Wolf Tracks on the Welcome Mat," published by Oreanabooks, an imprint of Carmel Publishing Company, and are used here by permission.

For permission to reprint lyrics of songs co-written with Paul Zarzyski, grateful acknowledgment is made to Ian Tyson for "Jerry Ambler," to Tom Russell for "Bucking Horse Moon," and "All This Way for the Short Ride," to David Wilkie for "Black upon Tan," to Wylie Gustafson for "Hang-'n'-Rattle," "Wicked Kiss," "The Mistress, The Maestro," "A Pony Called Love," and "Riding Double Wild,"and to John Hollis for "Maria Benitez."

Back cover photo of Paul Zarzyski at his desk courtesy of Kenton Rowe, www.kentonrowephotography.com.

Published in the United States by

Bangtail Press
P. O. Box 11262
Bozeman, MT 59719
www.bangtailpress.com

In loving memory of Leonard John Zarzyski—November 5, 1925 to October 10, 2008—and with gratitude to friends Maggie and Larry Biehl for their wise, consoling words during the most sorrowful moment of my life: "Show your father that you are strong and give him some credit for making you so. For him to die, he must know that you are prepared to go on living. If you do that, you will make him proud. And there is no greater gift a son can give his father." (Sept. 23, 2008)

Table of Contents

Foreword: A One-Two-Three Combination-Punch Response to
51 from Songwriter and Painter Tom Russell   *5*

Purgatory's Blue Debris (poems)

The Religion of Winter   *12*
Flowering   *14*
What's Sacred   *16*
How I Tell My Dad I Love Him   *18*
Time Travel   *20*
Photo Finish   *22*
What of the Ugly   *24*
Smart-Mouth: Mandibular Prognathism   *26*
Turkey Buzzards Circling Nirvana   *28*
Aftermath   *30*

Night is the Woman (lyrics)

God and Fear   *34*
Black Upon Tan   *36*
Riding Double Wild   *38*
A Pony Called Love   *40*
Bucking Horse Moon   *42*
Lucky Charms of Love   *44*
All This Way for the Short Ride   *46*

The Long Shot Gods (poems)

Labor Day   *50*
Smoke   *52*
As The World Turns   *53*
Sadly—Oh-So-Sadly—I Have to Explain *The Sopranos*... *54*
The Pummel and Pump, The Push, The Fix and The Trip *55*
Last Rematch   *57*
Good Friday   *59*
Jerry Ambler   *62*
In D. C. to Recite Cowboy Poems...   *64*
Fairy Tale   *67*

Buckin' Hoss Cocktails (lyrics)

Not a Lover, Not a Fighter 72
Jerry Ambler 74
Long Sagebrush Drives 77
Hang-'n'-Rattle! 79
Maria Benitez 80
Bob Dylan Bronc Song 82

Galloping Off A Cappella (poems)

Wondering Where the Blind Boy Goes at Night 88
And All the World Would Call Me "Rich" 90
Hard Traveling 92
Leaping None Too Soon into Lightness 93
Rubato: Stolen Time 95
Aces and Eights 98
How Near Viet Nam Came to US 100
Red Light 102
Snapshot Gravity 105
Watching the Sun Set Over Santa Fe—City of Holy Faith 107

Sweet Wicked Sin (lyrics)

No Forbidden Flowers 110
The Best Dance 112
The Christmas Saguaro Soiree 114
Wicked Kiss 116
Hope Chest 118
The Mistress, The Maestro 120
Roadwork in the Boneyard 122

5 Memoir Rounds with 1 Paul Zarzyski:
A Self-Interview 125

51

30 Poems
20 Lyrics
1 Self-Interview

Paul Zarzyski

A One-Two-Three Combination-Punch Response to *51* from Songwriter and Painter Tom Russell

Gary Snyder once listed—in "What You Should Know to Be a Poet"—the importance of knowing the names of trees and flowers and weeds...on down to "the wild freedom of the dance—ecstasy." Zarzyski knows all of this. And more. Deep research honed from hanging on the side of a bronc; on down to hanging onto what's left of your heart when your parents die. Close up. Unflinching. It's all here. Chain sawed from oak and maple; aged in Polish-Italian, veal-kidney gravy. The real deal. In the music world they keep harping on this thing called *Americana*. What could be more masterfully *Americana* than the poems, song lyrics, and self-interview composed herein by Paul Zarzyski? From "The Religion of Winter" to "Wondering Where the Blind Boy Goes at Night" and on through song lyrics and the self-interview, I am moved to the core. A rare occurrence.

The last time I was knee-walking drunk was in a little seafood joint on the end of the Monterey pier. Vodka tonics and Margaritas melted into bottles of Dago Red as the sea lions roared on adjacent docks and pelicans dove for grunion. I was "fine-dining" with the great *maestro-bards* Ian Tyson and Paul Zarzyski. Last thing I recall, *Lord*, was an Irish pub; Zarzo tossing Roberto Duran jabs at me as the Monterey Festival organizers skittered away with disapproving scowls. Zarzyski always takes it to the edge, then leaps over. He pulls us with him. Hunter Thompson territory. Writes the way he lives. Relentless. Deep. Passionate. In this new tome he lays heart and soul on the line with dispatches from his "robust world," saturated in North Wisconsin, Polish-Italian polenta and veal-kidney gravy. You can taste the words. The real *gen*. From the master. Poems, song lyrics, a self-interview. It's all here. It will *change* you. Great art *should*. It's rock and roll. It's righteous. *It sings* and sinks into your spirit, like that drunken and loving jab thrown at me in the Monterey night.

The Mexicans have a word, *gritando*, which is derived from the noun *grito*. An exuberant shout! A declaration of extreme joy or pain—perhaps celebrating drunkenness, love, or the coming of a revolution. Raising the roof or kicking up a fuss. A cry from the soul. Zarzyski's poetry, hell, *his very life's work*, always hits me like a loud and feral "*grito*" from the pen of this North Wisconsin, ex-pat, bard-cum-bareback bronc rider, cum-*poet*, in the best and oldest sense of that misused word. Zarzyski swings his fabled, double-bitted axe into the great American word trove, our *lingo*, and delivers finely-crafted short cords of poetic art, stacked neatly and tossed into our laps, with the blood from his knuckles and open veins shining on the split oak, maple, ash, and yellow birch. Blood gone thick on the pages. *Art*, they call it. Hail the master. Read this book. A little of the passion might rub off on all of us, and edge us toward the poetic redemption we need and crave.

Some degree of courage is in order if you wish to fully admit your life. You have to take a draught of ego poison to accept the full dimensions of your banality, your sheer corniness and ordinariness, the monstrous silliness of private ambitions and sexual fantasies, your loutish peacockery, your spates of sloth, all of which is to say that you were specifically not destined for the spiritual big time....

> Jim Harrison
> *Off To The Side: A Memoir*

...to try to learn from boxers was a quintessentially comic quest. Boxers were liars. Champions were great liars. Once you knew what they thought you could hit them. So their personalities became masterpieces of concealment.

> Norman Mailer
> *The Fight*

To move through pain to triumph—or the semblance of triumph—is the writer's, as it is the boxer's, hope.

> Joyce Carol Oates
> *On Boxing*

Purgatory's Blue Debris

The Religion of Winter

With my first glimpse of light, I felt the black-
hole swallower of stars—the enemy, death,
stalking the universe. Shooting my BB gun
at everything gleaming—songbird to pop bottle,
bullfrog to full moon—I squirmed,
against fear, to be a devil-may-care boy,
until my first Christian wake. There,
six years into life, I shivered
for my friend Mr. Stremski, the produce man,
displayed in a casket, his pallid cheeks
rouged lightly as the first trucked-in peaches
of the year. He'd given me carrot greens,
wilted lettuce, apples gone bad, and his magic
salve to kill the invisible mites
blistering my rabbits' ears. And when he'd heal
their black-scabbed membranes pink
again, I knew I'd take the breathing
worker of miracles, the living hero, any day,
over ten heavensful of dead saints.

With my fortieth autumn ebbing, I remember still
his interim depository, the mausoleum
like a meat locker outside
the graveyard's wrought iron fence—
earth, a white-knuckled fist
no god could pry open. That cold
storage of grief haunts me, from winter

to sudden winter. With October's arctic low,
the sky, like a tease, opens,
and swans, translucent beneath noon sun,
slice south before the river's final breath
against a lid of ice. I've grown to love their song
as I've come to love, more than Rock,
the Blues. My mother and father live
and I worship whatever luck or lore favors them
through another Wisconsin winter. They burrow-in,
contented to pray for the dead, yet
they cannot fathom why
I gather my firewood one day at a time,
why, defiant in shirt-sleeves, I scorn
the shortness of light through the screen door.

Flowering

Their rump hairs puffed, chrysanthemum
antelope blossom from beds
into morning hoarfrost, the rancid
scent of carnivore
boring through the tranquil
air of their world
turning, in a single whiff,
hostile.
      His rifle propped
solid, crosshairs fixed, melded
into the black-haired face, why
does this hunter, in awe of himself, stop
squeezing off the easy shot?
                      Not
because he's learned horned angels
germinate from earth
to save us from our own
cherubic ghosts—these animals
floating over rolling prairies of snow
like seraphim through cumulus.
                    Far less cosmic,
he stops because he feels his heart
refusing to march or charge
in uniform. At a pastoral stroll through rib
thicket—through flesh and Malone wool
and into a red-orange lichen coat
adorning the boulder

he's nestled against—the thrum of warm waves
pulsates back into him.
                              During this
nearly indiscernible blink
within his forty-fifth winter, he yearns
for the fine tendrils of silence
crystalline air clings to,
most vitally, right before the rifle
fires.
         This instant, sunshine,
burning off the frost,
ignites the snapshot into action
time-lapse-fast
toward a spring run-off
May morning on this very spot—antelope
browsing through wild iris and blue
lupine they all choose not to pick.

What's Sacred

To wake because waking means something,
something you're itching to begin
living at daybreak—revelry of autumn
cottonwood leaves, shod horses
clicking over scree, far-off
cacophony of meadowlark aria with crow
ruckus, goshawk skirl, strident magpie
cries breezed through a bedroom
window screen, tinkling wind chimes
echoing steeple bells
deep out of some distant
childhood dream.
                To hopscotch
or, better odds, slip-slip
succinctly into your jeans
with brisk whispers from each
instep thrust, fifty-plus
years of this denim
one-two gymnastic balancing act
on the high wire between
half-asleep and wide-awake—right leg
then left—ankles, knees, hips,
lumbar, *snap-crackle-popping*
their breakfast applause.
                To splash
well water into your prayerful hands, cotton-

towel your eyelids dry, focus,
voice with a joyous *ahhhh*
your first hot swallow of joe
kick-starting your ticker
before walking your Aussie dog,
Zeke, who loves you for your clockwork
newspaper fetchings
from that blue speck of a box, far
as the blue eye can see,
a long jaunt off.
            To inhale,
until your lungs flex like biceps,
canine windfalls of fresh scents, dry leaves
redolent in the night's wake, gold
certificates flushed from the sprung
back doors of an armored car, both
sagebrushed ditches
flitting with winged brilliance
crisp for the picking at 6 a.m.
when you shall be the only two in sight
eager enough to inherit,
breath after rich fertile breath, this earth.

For Ray and Barbara March

How I Tell My Dad I Love Him

Knocking down the standing dead
oak, maple, ash, yellow birch
in July humidity all day long, we
take a blow only to guzzle
spring water from moonshine jugs—
same jugs, same artesian seep, same
father and son who made wood
together one-half century ago, me at six
swinging a hickory double-bit
Dad carved as he whittled
into me the virtue of work, same pride
a blue-collar poet knows
sizing-up the ricks, the short cords of words,
split and fit into stacks
during another hard shift in the woods. Dad
gestures to me his slow-motion
coup de grâce—kill it, quitting time—
straight razor across the throat
Sicilian sign language with thick Polish finger
just as my chainsaw, racing
out of gas, bucks into two
matching sixteen-inch rounds
the butt-end of a fifty-footer
I was itching to finish. Flocked
with sawdust from my boot laces up
to the crown button of my Paul Bunyan ball cap,
I saunter to the stump
Dad sits on, The Lumberjack Thinker

pondering four score and two years of BTUs. He
does not see me peeling the heavy red
sweat-soaked t-shirt
inside-out up over my torso and face—
popping its collar, like a cork
out of a crock nozzle,
off my forehead. I toss it
splashing into his lap
with reptile heft. He jumps,
cusses me with a laugh, agrees
to replenish my Pabst Blue Ribbon reservoir,
replace my shredded gloves. Our deal
sealed with a handshake, ever so
less virile lately, tender as a hug,
we drive the same slow miles home—
dripping in the sweetest silence he knows.

For my brother, Gary

Time Travel

Gravel roads into a black hole
canopy of hardwood forest
were all the secrets of the cosmos,
all the signs of the zodiac,
she and I craved in those rock-and-roll days
before compact cars. We made aerobic love
in the king-size back seat of a '56 Buick
Roadmaster—pink Buck Rogers rocket ship
I flew with one finger locked
cool to the fuchsia suicide knob
while she clung so close
we exchanged our hearts' accelerated drum
solos like the last all-out heat
in a battle of the bands. Flying fast as
teenage foreplay to our favorite parking spot, high
beams nipping recklessly at the heels of risk,
we turned our eyes from the road
for a breathless kiss, miles long. It's been eons
since I've glimpsed the red needle's defiance
to the right, and now, climbing past 95,
rushing home the emergency serum
for the fevered mare that so easily foaled
but cannot slip her afterbirth—now,
with old thrills relived for this instant,
should I regret my childless years,
the way we dreaded pregnancy

back then, how we chanced sparking
new life in our quest to test death? What if
this speed today was for my own
flesh and blood anxious within
a young wife? What if this
two-lane pavement turned
abruptly into gravel—rooster tails of dust
churning in the rearview—rolling
prairie morphed into maple and oak forest,
and this daylight into just one more dark
night's play of rhythm-method
roulette around the old back road to Schumacher's
Park with her? Slowing down to 110,
I whisper *What love. What luck.* But
coming to a whiplash stop,
to the '71 Chev's engine ticking
Geiger counter-frenzied, I wonder
was it ever love at all, and if
it was, then how long, I ask,
does luck's half-life last?

Photo Finish

Because a horse cannot see its own nose,
the bell mare stares at herself
mesmerized in the mirrored glass
vet clinic door—fixates so firmly
she's distracted from her chronic pain,
her herd-bound angst, her equine
gender's, shall we say, *testiness*? Deaf
to the duct tape's reptilian hiss
ripping off the roll—the vet
figure-eighting both front Styrofoam-padded hooves—
Cody, lulled by a million cc's curiosity,
balances passively on three legs
until, almost one wing beat too soon, a finch,
flitting through her reflection, snaps
her out of her hip-cocked hypnotic trance back to
her fractious, pawing, snorting self
hell-bent to load up and haul home.
        Trailer
rocking a Richter-scale 6.8 on its hitch,
the Ford's flopping rearview tilts
just enough to force me to ponder,
glimpsing right, my own profile,
though, with one eye closed, *I can see*
purt-near around the prow of the nose
I've preferred all my life not
to regard too closely.
        Pushing fifty now,
I take my cues from wise old Cody,

thrice her twenty-five years. I decide this,
indeed, is a Triple Crown nose, a nose
with *run for the roses* written all over it—thick
antithesis of *aquiline*, or even *equine*,
yet still reaching far enough beyond my hat brim
to absorb healthy photonic doses of solar vitamin D,
to make each and every oxygen molecule
feel especially welcomed. It's that kind
of in-with-the-good, out-with-the-bad
nose that discerns, three blocks off,
fine cuisine from rancid grease,
alluring pheromones from cheap perfume,
music from boom box blare—our ears, admit it,
the worst of the five-senses-slackers
since the eyes accepted polyester.
                                             Nostrils flared,
rhinoplasty be damned, this is *thee* nose
for poetry, a prosodic nose, a nose that will
bulldog and bulldoze its way
to the flashbulb finish line of life
where that un-retouched snapshot will prove
aerodynamically-challenged me
The Winner.

What of the Ugly?

The ugly cannot buy into the World
of Disney's *Beauty and the Beast*. False
reflections in fun house mirrors, the ugly,
becoming gorgeously distorted, suddenly know
nothing about truth. Truth, you see,
blooms from the ugly looking it
square in the eye every time
they're caught off guard by chrome,
porcelain, Mop and Glo'ed linoleum,
lacquered furniture buffed
to a deep gloss finish, anything
behind or under glass. The ugly prefer dirty
cars not simonized to raindrop-
beaded sheens. They shy from clear water
moving slow or pooled. Adept
in geometry, the ugly will eyeball
precisely the angle at which
side- and rear-views will crop them
driving out of the picture. The ugly like
their silver tarnished, their glass smudged
or smoky, their sky cloudy. No *Vanity Fair*,
Cosmo., *Victoria's Secret*, *G.Q.*, ad infinitum
ever shine from the ugly's mail,
though they will at times risk the slick
photographs of *National Wildlife*, and love
Humane Society billboards reading
"Single Aussie female with whiskers, big nose,
hairy chest and one glass eye
seeking mate in the country." It's true

what the beautiful say about ugly
going "right to the bone"—the deeper
the glow below, the lovelier
to the ugly. They'd rather mine
the marrow for one moment—faceless
shadows ruling there and driving
the beautiful mad—than be blinded
by fluorescent light off the flawless
skin's surface. Did I mention the ugly
despising the wearers of those chic
mirrored sunglasses? Users of close-up
camera lenses? Dentists in general and, far worse,
myopic optometrists? The ugly go out of their way
to say the Lord's name in vain
while praying for parity in heaven or,
better yet, getting even
in hell. The ugly know
things will get much uglier, but we refuse to
fear death. We do not forget
our catechism. We have learned,
shaving or putting on our makeup,
how to stand before ourselves
in judgment, meeting daily, face-
to-face, the spitting image of God.

Smart Mouth: Mandibular Prognathism*

*A condition where the lower jaw outgrows
the upper—alleged to have been derived from
the *princely Polish* family of Mazovian Piasts.

Novocaine turning my face to stone, I learn
it's my last remaining wisdom
tooth Doctor Olsen is crowning
in porcelain—right side, right brain,
sanctum sanctorum, holy of holies,
the tabernacle, the cranial grail
frothing hot with creativity, and what is
creativity if not the infinite
rainbow bridge of wisdom between
body and soul? I'll gladly stroll
to my grave still grinding that day
whatever toil or torment
this perfect imperfect world
causes to stick in my craw, thanks
to the jut of my lower jaw,
my bulldog underbite
aligning my right upper
second molar with this
one bottom third molar
miraculously granted its sovereign stay
of execution on extraction day
decades back when Doc Odorizzi—army
airborne jumper of the Rhine
behind enemy lines and, thereafter,
deemer of fear as redeeming virtue—
must have incurred a lethargic lapse
into compassion.
                    Soft food be damned,
I plan to exit this earth chewing
still on life's hardtack,

flossing with coarse mane hair
of a bronc. I'm going out kicking,
spitting into the hurricane eye
of ignorance. I'll not bow to
fiction or fact, to all the ballyhoo
and foofaraw, the flimflamming boogeyman
humbuggery, or the sheep's wool
pulled over our eyeteeth by queens,
high priests, presidents, kings,
soothsayers, succubi or tooth fairies
scamming to snatch our last
molars from beneath death
bed's pillow soaked with drool,
with dreams unlived.
                            I will renounce Satan,
decay *and* gum disease. I'll gargle
daily with Mexican perfume—blue agave
tequila reposado—shower my wisdom
tooth in euphoric bright lights. I'll yodel
like a lone wolf rodeo poet soprano
extolling the arioso's holiest note,
my tongue tucked, head tilted back, crown
blinding with its brilliance
heaven's Mensa intelligentsia—them gaping
dumbfounded while regaling
in the scintillation of this royalty,
this Epicurean jewel, this *numero* thirty-two
virtuoso oracle holding court,
ruling the roost, cock-a-doodle-
dooing until closing time
my loftiest thoughts from its deep-
rooted, four-legged stool at the end of the bar.

For George and the Gang
And for Doc John Martin

Turkey Buzzards Circling Nirvana

Do not go gentle into that good night.
Rage, rage against the dying of the light.

Dylan Thomas

Anything that ain't got some fighting in it
is like a funeral, and I DON'T like funerals.

John L. Sullivan

I'm fed-up burying all my dead friends
never quite friend-enough to hang tough
long enough to haul my carcass off. Who'll be left
to honor my last sonsabitching wishes, to tell how
I abhorred, more than weddings, this
boring ceremony with its slow crawl—land-barge
caravan of traffic jam sadness
led by death's ebony stretch limo,
the world's most crooked cabby
rolling at the speed of greed, six-digit
jockeybox meter spinning a-blur
faster than reels of a one-armed bandit. Speaking of
highway robbery, of watching death dry, *if*
anyone *is* still around, make my final ride
person-flaked flamed. Stir my coarse ash
into thirty coats of lacquer
sprayed over the blazing
orange of both '40s Merc doors. Paint me
roaring with metaphorical fire
down some one-horse-town's quarter mile. Punch it
while passing paper-sacked pints
of high school wine. Bravado
and fuel tanks overflowing, cruise
Hell's drag with its one lurid stop light
beaming eternal, the grim reaper

glowering in the crosswalk. Screw him *and*
that Texas penknife he packs
in these computerized-nuke times. Swerve,
brush the anorectic booger back
to the curb—door him, moon him,
flip him off and leave him coughing
up his Hoover vacuum bag guts
in your burnt-rubber exhaust, your raucous
yee-HAW! At *my* final cash-in and last blast-off
I want you jaspers to laugh
so hard you almost die, but don't—I want to
leave you believing there might be just one
more wild good-bye like this to live for.

For Jim Rooney

Aftermath

In the year of our Lord, two thousand and one,
on Tuesday, September eleventh—Satan's finest
answer to the Sabbath in a long time—
I retreat, on the first day of the fourth war
during my fiftieth year on earth,
from religion, go AWOL, default, fold, quit,
cancel CNN coverage at Ground Zero. Unplugged,
I shovel heavy wet manure,
rake barn stalls, scrape corrals,
lean my 175 pounds into the wheelbarrow heaped high
as I heaped it in 1969, at 18, striving
too hard to impress the big boss
on the first day of my first five-buck-per-hour job
packing hod. Back then, I did not fear
fear itself, the devil, flying fast,
flags, casual sex, Viet Cong, the cold
war, prayer or mortal sin. Trying to shirk
the burden of it all, that one stark image
of the second jet sailing into shadowy view—upper
right corner of the screen—I ignore
my heart jackhammering
behind crosshatched steel of I-beamed ribcage,
behind concrete and glass, flesh and blood
of sternum heaving. In a cloud of horse manure
dust, my reservoir of tears—forced now
through the pores and falling dry—cannot temper
fires from Montana to New York. This sun bears down

on me and, it seems, only me,
blinded by my own sweat, and straining
against purgatory's blue debris
without end—without red
hell's bottom, or heaven's white top, in sight.

Night is the Woman

God and Fear

They say "the Rapture's coming"
I say "let the bastard come"
They say "Armageddon's gunning"
I say "I'm the faster gun."

They say "there's no denying"
I say "defy unto thy end"
They say "you'll be left behind"
I say " adios, my friends, amen."

>Me and Jesus in a pickup
>Going fishing, drinking beer
>Cruising through The Masterpiece
>Without guilt and without fear.

They tell me "read the Scriptures
The apocalypse is now
The Prince of Darkness grips us"
I tell them "Holy Cow!"

They tell me they're the chosen
The U.S. of J.C. choice
While their souls are decomposin'
Let our flesh and blood rejoice.

"Eye-for-eye and tooth-for-tooth"
They say "God won't reconcile"
I say "God *is* the light of mercy
With a twenty-twenty smile."

So me and Jesus, we go fishing
Talking creativity
"Praise Forgiveness" is his mantra
"Renounce Fear!" his decree.

Then me and Jesus, we go swimming
He's a fan of body art
BEING SCARED AIN'T BEING SACRED
Is tattooed above his heart.

God and *Fear* are two words,
Thank heaven, death shall part.

For Greg Keeler

Black Upon Tan

(with David Wilkie and Denise Withnell)

As she poured him a pint and a Tullamore Dew
He looked uninspired, and that's how she knew
He's adrift and he's bitter, on riptides of hate
On the sea of cheap whiskey toward Lucifer's gate.

At a shake-a-day pub, they call Pug Mahon's
In Billings, Montana, as he rattled the bones
Just 4,000 miles southwest of Dublin
A red-headed bartender taught him 'bout lovin':
      (when she said)

      "The Guinness caresses the Harp as you sip it
      Forgiveness, it blesses the heart, if you let it"
      She spoke as she floated the black upon tan
      "The night is the woman, the day is the man."

Her words rolling lovely as dice from the cup
"A Winner!" she shouted, as he finally looked up
Across the mahogany bar, her red hair
Like blood of the Irish, half fire, half prayer.

When an angel sails in, the Devil he runs
Three cheers to the Motherland daughters and sons
The green neon shamrock's wings taking flight
She taught him how darkness embraces the light:
      (when she said)

"The Guinness caresses the Harp as you sip it
Forgiveness, it blesses the heart, if you let it"
She spoke as she floated the black upon tan
"The night is the woman, the day is the man."

Forgiveness, it blesses the heart, if you let it.

For Wally and Ruthie

Riding Double Wild

(with Wylie Gustafson)

She's a motorcycle sister
He's a bareback bronc twister
They're riding double-wild 'cross the West
She's Mescalero Indian
He's full-blooded Paladin
Where they're going is anybody's guess.

    Cowboy grit, Apache pride
    Wild hearts will collide
    Rolling down the road, desperados in love
    The West is still wild as she ever was!

She drives that bike full-throttle
She's got a half-full bottle
Of mescal in her studded saddlebags
He spurs them buckers crazy
Now he's laid-back and lazy
Batwing chaps a-flapping just like flags.

She wears a Stetson with stampede strings
Skull and cross-bone earrings
Moonlight beaming off her buckrein braids
He slips on down behind her
Wraps his arms around her
Pop! Pop! Pop! sings that four-stroke serenade.

Pinto stallion, black and chrome
Painted metal, flesh and bone
Rev it up, pop the clutch, desperados in love
The West is still wild as she ever was!

Leather jacket skinny-dippers
Fingers swimming through her zippers
Whiskers rubbing up against her tattooed neck
Suicide shifting, weaving and a-drifting
What he whispers in her ear could cause a wreck.

Cowboy grit, Apache pride
Wild hearts will collide
Rolling down the road, desperados in love
The West is still wild as she ever was!

Ahhh, the West is still wild as she ever was!

A Pony Called Love

(with Wylie Gustafson)

Love bucked me off on the second jump out
With a suck-back twist, a squeal and a shout
It's a long swim back, no hope or applause
Through riptides and currents and a frenzy of jaws.

    She's a heartbreaker
    That pony called Love.

The last drops wrung from a valentine sponge
My blood must taste bitter on the tip of her tongue
No high moral ground, no place to hide
From the battle of tarantulas deep down inside.

    She's a heartbreaker
    That pony called Love.

        I've been hung-up, stepped on,
        Kicked in the heart
        She's a rank one come-apart
        She's a pony called Love.

So it's back down the road with my soul in a cast
Not a highway alive that don't lead to the past
As I sip from the go-cup of bottomless pain
I see demons in the headlights...or could they be saints?

She's a heartbreaker
That pony called Love.

Oh, she's a soul-taker
That pony called Love.

Bucking Horse Moon

(with Tom Russell)

Down a one-lane road, there's a dusty fairground
Where I learned the bronc trade and I fell in love
With a blue-eyed twister, and her smoky whisper
She said, "they call me the Cimarron Dove."

We'd spool our bedrolls on down together
My calloused hands combed through her hair
She'd stare at a star through an old mesquite tree
"See that moon shadow? There's a bucking horse there!"

> Sweet bird of youth, no easy keeper
> Flown with the seasons, all too soon
> Beneath Montana's blue roan skies
> Nevada starlight, and a bucking horse moon.

Our love reeled out like a western movie
Down heart-worn highways through the rodeo towns
Wrapped in her wings for the midnight flight
That bucking horse moon kept shining down.

> Bucking horse moon on the hood of the truck
> She'd smile and say "that means good luck"
> Bucking horse shadow through the purple sage
> "We'll ride forever, our love won't age."

But heart and bone are made for breakin'
The Cimarron Dove's flown with the wind
Then a bronc in Prescott rolled on my back
I'll never ride roughstock again.

Sweet bird of youth, no easy keeper
Flown with the seasons all too soon
Beneath Montana's blue roan skies
Nevada starlight and a bucking horse moon.

I lost my youth on the dusty fairgrounds
I'm an old bronc fighter long past high noon
But on a haunted night wind, I can hear her whispering
As I search the heavens for the bucking horse moon
The Cimarron Dove and the bucking horse moon.

Sweet bird of youth, no easy keeper
Flown with the seasons all too soon
Beneath Montana's blue roan skies
Nevada starlight and the bucking horse moon
Wyoming sundown and the bucking horse moon.

For Walt LaRue
and Ramblin' Jack Elliott

Lucky Charms of Love

(with Betsy Hagar)

Earth whispered through the gables
Wet sagebrush on Her breath
Mares nickered in their stables
The mysteries of the West
Raindrops on the cedar shakes
The angels' telegraph
Their message reads "make love," she'd say
He'd frown and they'd both laugh.

> Heaven in the hayloft
> As daylight disappears
> Wind chimes in the rafters
> Sweet music to their ears
> Twine and worn-out horseshoes
> They swing and pirouette
> The lucky charms of lovers
> One for every time they met.

Her daddy climbed the ladder
One windy summer day
Found the xylophone mobile
Laughed it off as child's play
That old barn will last forever
Wish her daddy could have too
But she still meets her husband there
And they hang another shoe.

Heaven in the hayloft
As daylight disappears
Wind chimes in the rafters
Sweet music to their ears
Gleam of twirling horseshoes
A hundred, maybe more
The bells of distant steeples
Ring from heaven's gabled door.

Lucky iron, shining cups
Silver heels, all pointing up
Little dippers, barely tipped
Keeping love from spilling.

A graveyard in the meadow
Where they'll both be laid to rest
Adorns the barn's long shadow
When the sun's low in the west
And when that evening zephyr
Stirs the shoes into a chime
They seem to ring most lovingly
In the heart of haying time.

Heaven in the hayloft
Lifetimes flying by
Starlight in the rafters
Sweet music to the eye
Galaxies of wind chimes
A western shrine to love
Where each angelic message
Sparked one new star above.

Heaven in the hayloft
And the lucky charms of love...

All This Way for the Short Ride

(with Tom Russell)

> "...It's impossible, when dust
> settling to the backs of large animals
> makes a racket you can't think in,
> impossible to conceive that pure fear,
> whether measured in degrees of cold
> or heat, can both freeze
> and incinerate so much
> in mere seconds...."

Well the chute gate swings open
Here we go again
The desperate dance
The kick and the spin
Dust rising from a crossbred bull
Fire meets with pride
A man comes a long way
Just for the short ride.

His wife's in the grandstand
Trying to swallow the fear
A little baby inside her
Whose time's drawing near
The bull flying higher now
Then he falls to his side
Their love came a long way
Just for the short ride.

Two hearts in the darkness
Sing a blue lullaby
Beat the drum slowly
For a cowboy's last ride.

When the dust it all settled
And the crowd disappeared
The sirens still echoed
In an unborn child's ear
The little boy's due in April
He'll have Daddy's blue eyes
He'll always remember
His father's last ride.

They preached at the service
From John 25
How Christ came a long way
Just for the short ride.

Beat the drum slowly
For a cowboy's last ride.

Well, the chute gate swings open
Here we go again....

*For Patty, and for "Little Joe" Lear
and Families*

The Long Shot Gods

Labor Day

"I came to America because I heard the streets
were paved with gold. When I got here I found
out three things: first the streets were not paved
with gold, second they weren't paved at all, and
third, I was expected to pave them."
Italian Immigrant Quote—
Ellis Island Museum Wall

I spent my muscular blue-collar youth
pounding, prying, digging, lifting, hauling
ass for some wanna-be-god
boss who tallied-up the solid gold
hours of my prime, multiplied them
by a pittance, and pegged me
a hooked-in-the-gullet bottom-feeding
sucker for life.
                    Since, I've seen the lucre-green
Statue of Liberty up close, felt a chill
on Ellis Island where I strolled
the processing plant of my ancestors
off the boats from Italy,
from Poland, found Zarzycki, the old-
country spelling on the wall
and thought of soldiers first
setting foot in Nam.
                    Work is war
when it's work punched in and out of
solely for the sake of making wages
to pay the sticker price
some stranger places on your dream

always a dollar out of reach. And war is never
won.
        This land is our land, alright,
and these words are my words,
not for money, but love. I sweated blood,
labored all day, have the calluses
on my heart, the rock-hard
broad shoulders of the poet's soul
to show for them.
                As my ironic father,
rowing his bass boat over ferrous waters,
cracked wise to a young son on the one Monday
morning he was free of the iron
ore mine toil all year, now I—
alone in the mist of these lines cast
wistfully into the shallows—also wonder
"what *are* the poor people doing today."

For Tom Russell
In tribute to his "immigrant song
cycle" masterpiece, The Man from
God Knows Where

Smoke

Beneath the green neon **VACANCY**,
cottonwood leaves swirl
around the lawn chair
she lolls in, Indian summer
Friday afternoon, not one car
parked in the square
harbor of faded pink rooms
she has just finished cleaning
is what I surmise driving by this
1952 Route 66 flashback, her in light
wool plaid jacket, jeans, sneakers, lipstick, red
thick hair the wind can barely lift
ever-so-slightly. She is thin
because her life, and little else, graces her
thin, ageless, at ease
with her reflection in glass, this job
she has worked forever, each day
measured by the one cigarette break
she savors most—not at all too deep
in thought, yet so radiantly alone
among the yellow leaves
bustling like servants about her.

For Quinton Duval

As The World Turns

Conceived in northern Italy, a mountain town,
my mother crossed the Atlantic, 1920,
in the womb, lived her first twenty-seven years
at 507 Poplar Street, married
a navy man turned iron ore miner,
moved to 505 and stayed
married to the same man on the same street,
never learned to drive,
seldom missed Sunday mass or Friday fish
fries at the V.F.W. or Legion Hall,
raised three boys—prayed, cooked, cleaned house,
washed clothes, shopped for groceries—loved
The Mitch Miller and Lawrence Welk shows,
listens still to her polka
program, Saturday morning on WJMS,
while baking biscotti, doing something useful, she
having confessed to her poet son,
on her eightieth birthday, that she'd much
rather scrub *her* kitchen floor than read a book
because she just can't stand to just sit
and do nothing, except for tuning in
weekday afternoons to the everlasting soap
opera saga she's referring to
when she says, with so much joy in her voice,
"time to watch my story,"
though, not so oddly at all,
it's the farthest thing from it.

For Mom, on her 81st birthday—
November 20, 2001

Sadly—Oh-so-Sadly—I Have to Explain The Sopranos *to Someone Who Just Does Not* Capice

...you got it yet, *goomba*? I'm Eye-talian
and what we Eye-talians do, see,
besides communion with the one and only
true God, who also just so happens to be
EYE-talian—"Vengeance is mine
sayeth the lord?" Therefore we DID
invent the vendetta? —what we do,
we Eye-talians, is turn *sad*
into *mad*. That's our solemn calling, that's just
the way it is, see—*sad* into *mad*, but THEN
mad into *glad*. And *glad* is when we eat!

Which is all to say we work goddamn hard
at being sad. It's simple logic—bah-dah-boom,
bah-dah-bing. No sad, no mad. No mad,
no glad. No glad, no *mangia*! And we
all live to *mangia*, am I right or am I right?
Good! You finally got it! It looks like
maybe I won't have to kill you after all
'ey? I'm so glad—"pass the polenta!"—I'm SO
goddamn glad, *paesan*. Now let's eat
and pray before we do for something sad
to make us mad, again, by supper.

The Pummel and Pump,
the Push, the Fix, and the Trip

Autumn puts its overnight kibosh
on summer, buckles the hot
August knees with a crisp hook
to the liver, a definitive *i*-dotting
body shot, then drops it
with a sockdolager to the jaw. Rocked,
summer does the sunfish-
tossed-on-the-dock death
rattle flop. I, quivering, bones
chattering with thrill, lust after this
socked-in morning, thick air
pungent with whiffs of the unpicked
edible inky caps—words stirred
so near I can catch the staccato ticking
of my Muse's red stiletto heels, Her hubris
as She takes Her blue-bile, not
nubile, vitriolic time back to daddy,
traipsing Her way, making me pay
in diamond-studded spades, in clubbed hearts,
for months of neglect. I, writhing now,
suffer Her comeuppance like a smack
addict locked with bucket,
blanket, bunk, and cold-turkey ghost
screaming from a windowless turret. All
I need, baby, please—*pretty
please*—baby, is one thin line,

albeit feeble, or even just two
ruby syllables, elbows hitched
symphonically in sync—a tease, a taste,
a sliver of sour cream raisin pie
a la mode with macadamia nut sprinkles
topped with a dollop
of something chocolate, devilish, a little
tiny slice of how, true or not,
I believe it used to feel
smothered in your dark, lithe arms, my face,
my spent brain pressed
between bicep and breast. Smothered—
yes, *smothered*—in your musky scent, I want
poetry's musical perfume worked deep,
the morning after, into my pores,
into the sweetest cells of my honeycomb
lungs—so deep, I don't care
if ever I breathe real air again.

Last Rematch

Blood is like champagne to a fighter.
Al Lacy

Christmas eve in an 8-by-8 cellar,
he works the heavy bag, pummels
against pain of a chopping right
hand over the heart. He tries to go on loving
like a punch-drunk, legs long gone,
who cannot quit the ring, who cannot forget
the few rounds he won big.
                    In the corner,
rusty milk can for a stool,
he slumps, chin to chest,
forearms crossing his thighs
with dead weight he feels deep
to the femurs. He watches sweat beads drip
then hang in tangles of chest hair—
ornaments gleaming silvery
in the 60-watt. He wheezes and coughs
beneath the rickety gallows, thick dust
swarming in the squawking
friction of swivel joint to eyebolt, the bag
still swinging from a joist.
                    Among onions
hung in bunches to dry and hard

salamis aging, among pint Mason jars of plums,
apricots, sweet pickles, tomato sauce—
warm colors of summer she preserved
years ago—among shadows
the heavy bag throws, among ghosts
of Christmases past, he'll rise, jab,
jab-hook, uppercut, jab-jab, and hope
this round to hammer the body,
catch his second wind, dance,
dance his way out of her clinches.

Good Friday

I'd be goddamned glad to call it *Good*—
Good or, hell, even **Great**
with a bold capital **G**, if only
my capital-F Father,
celebrating the passion of the Apostles
was still here capital-F Fishing
today. Six vacant months ago,
Dad vanished and, far as I know, has not
glanced back, has not yet
semaphored to me, in dreams
of tempestuous Limbo, where he's anchored,
making camp, weathering and waiting out
the postmortem storm.
                 Melding into the fog bank
horizon on the other side, my dad left
dovetailed in his wake
one bird's-eye maple tackle box
half-filled with the cinder of a man
whose blue-collar hands loved
the smooth, slow-stroked
strumming of exotic grains he milled,
sanded, lacquered—enticed
into the light.
           For Lent, I gave up
betting on the long shot gods. Irony,
however, running amok and roughshod,

lording it over us, I still count on chance
collisions with kindred senses from some next
orbit, trek, quest, spin—some round
slippery wet stone I'll leap to
from this one I'm pirouetting upon
now in my needle-toed boots.
                                    The whirling
turbulence of bullet-proof youth
wanes daily. Waving pink flags
of uncertain surrender, I'm burdened
further and further by the deafening
vespid drone of capital-D Death
vexing, tormenting me
toward the lip of the abyss
before delivering its venomous shiv,
its shimmering drip of utmost vertigo.
                                    As sure
as some Cosmic Force created green apples bobbing,
I will cross—boulder by slick-mossy-backed-
rolling boulder—the far dark water,
thanks not to seas parting
but to the thick backs of fish,
to my Father's piscivorous spring itchings
from all six directions. I will listen
along the way, listen for the whistling
monofilament lines, maybe glimpse

his silver minnow lures, shooting stars
cast into the black from our Lonesome
Lake rowboat toward shore, the unknown,
toward the shallows, the boiling
siege of heavy feeders
wreaking havoc in the weeds.
                              I will plead
humbly for nothing—not miracle,
not mercy, not the unearned
inheritance of heaven's eternal bliss
invented on behalf of the dead
to mollify the living. Prayerless
with faith, I will launch
my lucky bait into the mystery
riddled with apparitions. I will keep vigil,
lean with the weight of all my heart
into the fogged mirror, my hands splayed,
fingers flattened against the glass,
against the murky depths. Mesmerized,
I will yearn until I fiercely see again
someone here I can love to believe in.

Jerry Ambler

Your marker with its bucking horse twister
carved in marble, with gold-buckle words
World Champion Saddle Bronc Rider 1946
facing Blue Mountain outside Monticello, Utah,
would move anyone who's ever craved
with every gritty molecule of his make-up
a winning spur ride—cocked his hammer,
nodded for the gate, marked one rocketing out,
fought for holts and felt every 1300-pound
ounce of quick and hard and sinewy
swordfish ballerina between his knees.

You don't know me, Ambler, from Adam's off-ox
and even if you could, times these days change
too drastically to say maybe we'd have driven
the same Cadillacs or Hudsons between pitchin's,
savored the same label of rye chased with dames
you'd no-doubt be unspooling your bedroll beside
before I could even reach my "how-do-ma'am"
John B. hat brim—handsome, tan, lusty,
grinning booger that you were in *Life*
and *Look* magazine Chesterfield Cigarette ads.

You bet, Jerry, only a damn fool palavers to the dead,
but I savvy, here and now, how the West
I've come to love bucks-on in the wild
blood passing through some porous red sandrock
canyon wall of time between your ride and mine.
I feel its *rounder* pulse still pounding
behind Powder River bucking chutes. I hear—
decades past my rodeo prime, as I slip
this shiny fifty-cent-piece into the slot
between marble and parched earth—Ian Tyson
resurrecting your story in a ranahan rap
forking beauty with truth, the old sittin' new,
solid as gospel in the roughstock middle.

For Ian, and for Cort Feeley

In D. C. to Recite Cowboy Poems for a Show Titled Poets, Politicians, and Other Storytellers, I Visit the Vietnam Veterans' Memorial and the Smithsonian Aerospace Museum, Back-to-Back

From a distance, solid black,
a Rorschach test figure
flashed fast, the winged and ghostly
silhouette of a stealth bomber,
not one rivet glimmering—nothing human,
nothing errored—no single components, no flaw,
not one weak link. It's another story up close.
After walking for hours the five-hundred-foot-long Wall
jeweled with youthful names
of fifty-eight thousand one hundred and eighty-three
so far, I look up from the butt-end
of a Minuteman missile, blank
save for the big white good-guy letters
U.S. and Utah manufacturer's *made-by* label,
as if we were talking Monkey Ward's slacks,
a placard of ballistics
like a tag telling us the size
is 70 feet by 39 ton. It's even harder
to fathom the 8,000-mile range
than it is to believe Mitsubishi,
maker of my VCR, built the Zero
from scrap we sold the Japanese cheap, or
to buy the Warren Commission's fiction

that reads Lee Harvey was a lone
assassin, just like Jack
slew the giant and got the goose
because mom threw his *magic-bullet*
beans out the window—all akin
to the tall tall tale that out in the cosmos long long ago
carbon, hydrogen, oxygen, and nitrogen
in a chain collision locked bumpers,
Alakazam, Fee-Fi-Fo-Fum, and BINGO
"heeere's Johnny!" Not "Johnny comes marching
home again, hurrah, hurrah,"
but Johnny who watched his TV
heroes pack pearl-handled .45's,
Johnny who loved
seeing action a mere decade before
he was drafted to kill V.C. in The Nam,
before his name here in D.C. became
a still-shot on the big black screen,
no picture moving, nothing silver
as the Lone Ranger's bullet coming
guaranteed-to-wing-but-never-kill,
a far cry from this
ballistic missile living—like the Wall,
underground—a rifle-shot away
from the back door of my home
in Montana. How many silos,
how many Walls can a honeycombed planet hold
before it collapses and implodes? And what if
one warhead struck close enough
to blow this memorial to bits? Who would
find Johnny Thorn, a name in jagged stone,

floating weightlessly in some black hole
and how would they know
he wasn't really Johnny Thorn *berg*? Or maybe
you'd believe the zillion pieces
would jigsaw together, Alakazam
again in outer space? If so,
let me tell you my cowboy rhymer
about the time I rode the great bronc
Widow-Maker to his knees
while I wolfed a sackful of popcorn,
never spilling one kernel
out into the wild blue yonder.

Fairy Tale

First, pity the astrophysicist, adrift
billions of light years away
from observatory earth—yearning
to explicate the deep
hidden meaning of the heavens' epic,
feeling his illiterate way
through the cryptic black-on-black script
of *dark matter* ciphers.
                                    Back to terra firma,
now picture the little African-
American girl in pigtails, cotton
floral-print dress and bobby socks. Say it's cherry
blossom season in DC. She is
learning to read and to write, she
is loving her history lessons
in school, she is having fun on Easter
vacation in our nation's capitol
where she stares up in awe—her dark eyes,
uncharted stars—at the white marble
statue of President Lincoln, at the colossal
alphabet letters of his
Gettysburg Address. In phonics
she has learned to enunciate
each word—ALL MEN ARE CRE-
A-TED E-QUAL.
                        The little girl thinks about
her blind friend back home. Older,

she might correlate the enormous
letters carved in stone
to a gargantuan braille that should touch
even the blindest-hearted. She does not know yet
how polemics, mixed with politics and civil war,
freed her great-great-grandparents. She's enchanted
with the giant white man in his giant white chair
gazing down upon her as she now gazes
at the new copper penny sinking slow
to the bottom of the Reflecting Pool,
heads up, as she'd hoped
it would rest, the face of Mr. Lincoln
radiant in the middle of her
calm reflection.
                    She recites
"Star Light, Star Bright
First Star I see tonight…"
articulating each syllable with a wish
she'll keep secret—something about the blind,
about letters she's learning to shape
across the page, about darkness
holding hands, at play, with light
to make all good
words in this whole wide world
once upon a time
simply shine.

For Kathy Ogren

Buckin' Hoss Cocktails

Not a Lover, Not a Fighter

While he measures off his buck rein
He's fighting off his deepest pain
When the chute gate opens wide he'll find relief
Viet Nam and Special Forces
Viet Cong and three divorces
No more war—aboard these horses he's at peace.

The anthem's not his favorite song
He's done believing in King Kong
He pledges his allegiance to lost youth
He's the old man on the circuit
Pushing 50 and he looks it
But the look of things is often far from truth.

> Not a lover, not a fighter
> Not a wild west bronc rider
> Not a notch carved in a six-gun
> For each time he sits one tall
> Not a lover, not a fighter
> Not a hero, he's much wiser
> Making every spur-lick count
> For one name on The Wall.

The clown act with its cannon blast
Will make him jump back to the past
Where he earned a purple heart and silver star
Someone said he hawked his medals
For entry fees and won that buckle
Shining bright from his dark corner of the bar.

He tips his hat to cheering crowds
It makes him sad and makes him proud
No one showed to cheer him home from Nam.
In peaceful sleep, sweetly dreaming
Snorty broncs and not men screaming
He finds beauty in the storm before the calm.

> Not a lover, not a fighter
> Not a wild west bronc rider
> Not a notch carved in a six-gun
> For each time he sits one tall
> Not a lover, not a fighter
> Not a hero, he's much wiser,
> Making every spur-lick count
> For one friend on The Wall.

He finds hope in those 8 seconds
When the only call that beckons
Is the cowboy code—ride 'em high and tight
Charging hard in his bronc saddle
He's distracted from his battle
As he's learning how to win without the fight.

As he's learning how to live without the fight.

Jerry Ambler

(with Ian Tyson)

Outside of Monticello
In the land of the Utes
Where you made your last run
Jerry Ambler
May your bloodline live on
In the red rocky buttes
The call of the wild
To rodeo ramblers.

World saddle bronc champion
Nineteen and forty-six
Pass the hat, boys, he's gone
Jerry Ambler
We're goin' to carve him a marker
With classic spur licks
So they'll know here lies the great
Jerry Ambler.

       Hang, rattle, and fire
       Stay clear of the wire
       Sometimes there ain't time for good-byes
       Dance fast down the middle
       To the Devil's hot fiddle
       Saint Peter ain't givin' rerides.

Down diamondback rattlesnake highway
To the site of your crash
May you lure them all in
Jerry Ambler
If tombstones were neon
What words would they flash
To those God-fearing
Swashbucklin' gamblers?

From Shiprock to Dillon
In their old 8-banger cars
May they stop by your grave
Jerry Ambler
If they knew heaven's brand
The fine print of the stars
What would they learn from them old
Roughstockin' gamblers?

> Dance close to the women
> Don't worry 'bout sinnin'
> Someday she'll all be long gone
> Nod your head, make a ride
> The ol' reverend lied, boys,
> There's no rodeoin' beyond.

Beneath ol' big Blue Mountain
May the wolves of the west
Howl over your bones
Jerry Ambler
And though rodeo cowboys
Never find rest
May your grave speak the truth
To these ramblers.

World saddle bronc champion
Nineteen and forty-six—
Pass the hat, boys, he's gone
Jerry Ambler
We're goin' to carve him a marker
With classic spur licks
So they'll know here lies the great
Jerry Ambler.

Hang, rattle, and fire
Stay clear of the wire
Sometimes there ain't time for good-byes
Dance fast down the middle
To the Devil's hot fiddle
Saint Peter ain't givin' rerides.

Dance close with the women
Don't worry 'bout sinnin'
Someday she'll all be long gone
Nod your head, make a ride
The ol' reverend lied, boys,
There's no rodeoin' beyond.

There's no rodeoin' beyond...

Jerry Ambler

Long Sagebrush Drives—A
Polish-Hobo-Rodeo-Poet-Rap

Six roughstock buck-offs in a land-barge Ford
Six riggin' bags cached in the trunk
Umpteen go-'rounds, none of us scored
Our riggin's all leaked and we sunk—

With our ids and our egos all shrunk
We're bummered in a deep purple funk.

Hatful-o'-ones buys a full tank-o'-gas
Sack-o'-chew-'n'-a-two-pack-o'-beer
The good news is while five guys crash
One half-awake feller can steer—

Just punch him into Copenhagen gear
He'll forget about sheep and count deer.

> Six roughstock Trekkies on a Galaxy trip
> On our starry-eyed Enterprise
> We're doing Warp 8 on **LSD**—
> Takin' Long Sagebrush Drives
> Talkin' Long Sagebrush Drives.

Six roughstock winners in a one-horse town
Fort Knox in a twenty-buck room
Rosined-up hot testosterone
Leather-'n'-Libido perfume—

Tip your lid with its bird-of-prey plume
At The Casanova Cowboy Saloon.

Summers of love on the rodeo trail
Groovin'-to-LeDoux-rock-'n'-rowel
High-octane buckin' hoss cocktails
Jacked-up on the Wolfman's howl—

With the yellow-moon-eyed hoot owl
See a Peckinpah *Wild Bunch* prowl.

      Six roughstock rounders orbiting the West
      Like nectar bees circling hives
      On our sweet-tooth quest for **LSD**—
      Takin' Long Sagebrush Drives
      Talkin' Long Sagebrush Drives
      When and where, but no whys
      On our Cowpoke Cosmos highs
      Across tie-dyed sunset skies. . .

      Takin' Loooonnngggg Sagebrush Drives.

Hang-'n'-Rattle!

(with Wylie Gustafson)

Aristotle, Plato, Jung and Freud
Were philosophizing good ol' boys
But the gist of all their words of wisdom
Begs the quintessential western question:

   Did you come to ride? Or did you come to hide?

Big talk comes cheap from a padded bar stool
But the roughstock gods don't suffer no fools
Sundown, Steel, Pickett, and Brown
Watchin' every move as you screw yourself down.

   Did you come to ride? Or did you come to hide?
   Did you come to ride? Or did you come to hide?
   Make up your mind now.

      You're born on the back of a high spinnin' rock
      Life's winding down with each tick of the clock
      Well it's high time, brother, you let it Hang-'n'-Rattle!
      Let 'er Hang-'n'-Rattle!

Crack the bomb bay doors and feel the wind a-whippin'
Fan a mega-tonner like ol' Slim Pickens
Fire in the heart, fire in the hole
Smokin' explosions of rodeo soul.

   Did you come to ride? Or did you come to hide?
   YEEEE-HAWWWW!

   Did you come to ride? Or did you come to hide?
   Did you come to ride? Or did you come to hide?

For Ted Waddell and Lynn Campion

Maria Benitez

(with John Hollis)

A bucking horse-twisting Gypsy
Trailing the moon to each show
I'm drawn to Maria's arena
In the piñons of New Mexico.

Her castanets, they telegraph passion
Her Spanish heels are a-Gatling gun quick
Like the fast ratchet sound of my rowels spinning 'round
And the ricochet ring when they click.

> *Viva* Maria Benitez
> *Ole*! Maria *Ole*!
> *Tu Estampa Flamenca*
> *Mi alma tan bronca*
> Like a stampede through ol' Santa Fe
> Ole! Maria Ole!

Flamenco, *Gitano*, the Gypsy
The stage is her own Loving Trail
She's cool as a matador dancing
To a high Andalusian wail.

And I ride on the wind of her rhythm
With her dance in my veins I can't lose
And I crave the bronc's fury and fire
The wild flame that we can't refuse

Viva Maria Benitez
Ole! Maria *Ole*!
Tu Estampa Flamenca
Mi alma tan bronca
Like a stampede through ol' Santa Fe
Ole! Maria *Ole*!

I'll ride with her soul for 8 seconds
Each muscle a-rippling like hers
And I'll sing to her hoof-pounding tempo
This love song that trills from my spurs.

Viva Maria Benitez
Ole! Maria *Ole*!
Tu Estampa Flamenca
Mi alma tan bronca
Like a stampede through ol' Santa Fe
Ole! Maria *Ole*!

Viva Maria *Ole*!
Ole! Maria *Ole*!

Bob Dylan Bronc Song

I rode the bronc Whiskey Talks
In the same arena Dylan sang
"Simple Twist of Fate"—
Bucking chutes on hallowed ground
Big gray stud-horse skyward bound
Where Bob in cowboy-hatted crown
Rode hard his concert stage.

I rode the bronc Whiskey Talks
In the same arena Dylan sang
"Like a Rolling Stone"—
Key of C with jazzy licks
Stopwatch clicking all 8 ticks
My spur rowels reached for cosmic kicks
Out in the Music Zone.

I rode the bronc Whiskey Talks
In the same arena Dylan sang
"Knockin' on Heaven's Door"—
Risk it all for just one song
Some losing's right, some winning's wrong
This ride might last the whole night long
A buckle if you score.

I rode the bronc Whiskey Talks
In the same arena Dylan sang
"All the Tired Horses"—
They cheered us from the bleacher pews
The organ groaned communion blues
I gave the nod, they lit the fuse
With atomic torches.

I rode the bronc Whiskey Talks
In the same arena Dylan sang
"John Wesley Hardin"—
Gunfighter of a by-gone time
Pistols sing and bullets rhyme
Church bells in the village chime
When heroes are departin'.

I rode the bronc Whiskey Talks
In the same arena Dylan sang
"Forever Young"—
Old hearts beating in reverse
Lady Luck in see-through skirt
Music's blessings, music's curse
God's songs forever sung.

> Though I've hung up my bareback riggin'
> The roughstock days are far from dead
> Bob Dylan's out there still a-giggin'
> And I'm here slinging words like lead.

Poetic souls still buck unbroken
A bronc is but a song unsung
Guitar picks and spurs a-strokin'
The desperado West un-won.

I rode the bronc Whiskey Talks
In the same arena Dylan sang
"Every Grain of Sand"—
Plug the juice into acoustic
Beat the drum until you bruise it
A pound of flesh, a pound of music
The blood, the bone, The Band.

I rode the bronc Whiskey Talks
In the same arena Dylan sang
"Blowing in the Wind"—
How many shows, how many broncs
How many two-bit honky-tonks
One-half sloshed and one-half zonked
Forgive us if we've sinned.

I rode the bronc Whiskey Talks
In the same arena Dylan sang
"Shelter from the Storm"—
Twin universes parallel
Which one's heaven, which one's hell
Two sisters kissing at the well
Mankind lacks a quorum.

I rode the bronc Whiskey Talks
In the same arena Dylan sang
"Hurricane"—
Old Bill Pickett dogs a bull

While Strange Fruit hangs in orchards full
Pure hatred with its downward pull
A far, *far* cry from *Shane.*

I rode the bronc Whiskey Talks
In the same arena Dylan sang
"Thunder on the Mountain"—
Youth ain't wasted on the young
No Holy Grail need touch their tongue
They'll drink up truth if truth is sung
Straight out of The Fountain.

   Though I've hung up my bareback riggin
   The roughstock days are far from dead
   Bob Dylan's out there still a-giggin'
   And I'm here slinging words like lead.

   Poetic souls still buck unbroken
   A bronc is but a song unsung
   Guitar picks and spurs a-strokin'
   The desperado West un-won.

I rode the bronc Whiskey Talks
In the same arena Dylan sang
"Lay, Lady, Lay"—
Don't need no re-rides of the past
No flags a-flyin' at half-mast
I pledge allegiance to what lasts
There's nothing more to say.

Again, For Tom

Galloping Off A Cappella

Wondering Where the
Blind Boy Goes at Night

To a virtuoso playing acoustic harp
in Guadalajara's *Camino Real*, we order gourmet
meals costing 80,000 pesos,
drink Margaritas among the jet set, and all
I can think about is the blind boy
above Lake Patzcuaro. His eye sockets looked
as if they'd just stopped smoldering, black
slits I could see
only when he lifted his head to play
his beat-up concertina
on the steep cobblestone street. Maybe someone
placed him there out of love
each day in the rickety chair,
plastic lard tub squeezed
between his knees. He slumped, clinging
to the music box like a buoy,
straining to hear, above fiesta
laughter and mariachi trumpet blast
from the plaza below, the approach
of sandaled feet, leather-soled
music to his ears. Strings of tourists
trudging uphill, through his world muted by sneakers,
veer around him in a wide arc
on their way to the *artesanias*
shops where they'll pay top dollar
for colors that flare. He waits,

wishing for their footsteps, their murmur
and wheeze of their pursiness—his cue to play
the only tune he knows. He played it twice
as I scrimped from my pocket
five one-hundred peso coins, not enough
to tip the harpist for a single chord,
nor buy one bite of fine cuisine. To swallow
amid the cold silver and crystal,
I close my eyes, try to believe
his cheek is warmed by candle glow at home
where the blind boy feasts on dreams of light.

And All the World Would Call Me "Rich"

If for one night I could be the man
embracing the big Martin Guitar, I would
wear a good guy's white hat, brushed
tweed jacket sporting rotund buttons
of gentle leather, and a cotton shirt
sans pearl snaps, sans starch. I would dress
as softly as possible, put some pounds on
around the middle, pawn the silver buckle I won
riding broncs, shave close twice
daily. I would relocate my poetry
pen to a hip pocket—not one coarse edge,
sharp heartbeat, belabored breath ever
coming between us. For even a single set,
if I could be the man caressing
that big Martin Guitar, I would dare to pluck
an angel's breast feather for a pick. I would
turn the tuning keys as piously
as Monsignor Prock unlocked the tabernacle
holding the hosts for high mass—an old jeweler,
eyes long gone, slow-waltzing
the tumblers to his grandfather's safe
telegraphing, through the smooth brass knob, secrets
only his fingertips can hear. For one breathstop

of a Zen moment, if I could just be
the man strumming the big Martin
Guitar, I would revel in every chord
extol each note. I would
marvel at the debut of all
blue flickerings on the sweet extreme
of music's universe, where I would travel
the six rails of light
shining up the neck, over the frets
toward what most folks want so bad
to call "God"—what the man, bowing his head
in the presence of the big Martin
Guitar he plays, calls "Grace."

For Rich O'Brien and Buck Ramsey

Hard Traveling

begins with our first drumrolled jump
out of the womb into the world of air
or water, into the days-old,
weeks-old, months- and years-old
rapid guitar-riff crescendo
toward our so-called peak
performance of our so-called prime,
not, if we are lucky—real lucky—
waning in the very same breath
but, instead, slowly into the day-
by-day, heartbeat-per-clocktick
deceleration of a lifetime
of breathing millions of conscious breaths,
each one, each unique one, a bronchial work
of beauty we keep secret, silent,
hidden from the world,
save for the most intimate
encounters with liquid or cold,
friend or foe or lover or god,
embracing us so firmly in arms
tender yet callous, frightful yet soothing—
so worthy of knowing what we know, we lay bare
all our magic, our miracles, all
the musical truths we are made of
before we move on.

For George Harrison

Leaping None Too Soon into Lightness

A settler having to set
the heaviest most cherished
heirloom along the trail
to some promised land, prairie
schooner sunk hubs-deep in mud,
oxen spent, anthems drenched, heart-
strings limp and soggy, yet not
altogether prayerless, I will arrive—
who knows where—whittled
down to sinew on my sixtieth,
helixes of tame shavings
whisked away in a birthday gale, riotous
dance in my every robust atom,
every molecule of lean
musical being, not one chaotic plod
left in my step, all lift,
all fabulous leap. I will be
salubrious, insouciant—big
muscular words perched in gondolas
of hot-air balloons, higher,
higher even than I believed at sixteen
I would forever drift free. Because
now, at fifty-six, I deconstruct
the metaphorical keepsake

Conestoga wagon bones—no reverse gear,
no rearview, tongue rotted, axles sagged—
collapsed and scattered out back, useless
as the tuned piano to the Sioux
warrior who spotted it from afar
sunk to its mahogany skull,
to its last sad glistening grimace, in gumbo
hardened by wind—this
odd symbol of loss
spooking both horse and Indian
brave, circling in, snorty,
awestruck, filled with song and thus
galloping off a cappella.

For Denise Withnell

Rubato: Stolen Time

A lop-sided heart beating
from the lodgepole pine wall it hangs on
to the right of my poetry-writing desk—
beating its expected calibrated beats
decades, eons, on the same battery—
the yellow birch burl clock
my dad's big hands
crosscut-sawed, sanded, anointed,
christened with movement,
clicks most emphatically
at daybreak. It—and the furnace
kicking-in, and my loud swallowing
of scalding coffee over the rough
raw lump in my throat—
strikes up that hard rock song
I falsely waltzed to this past
winter's tormented mornings
when I concocted any sweet reprieve
that would give me shelter
from death's noise.
                    I've pondered
far too long the smoky
clamor right after
the heart's fireworks grand finale
fades to acrid dark—one more

splash of punctuated black
detonated from a Jackson Pollock
canvas titled, let's just say,
The Infinity of Night.
                              I know nothing of
sequels, encores, postscripts,
altered states in the wake
of our last systolic starburst of blood
into the arteries. The visceral
aftermath of sadness, nevertheless,
becomes more my bailiwick
with age.
                    Embracing Dad once
again last night in a long good-bye,
I cried real tears
from deep within a dream. I woke
winded, exhausted, straining still
against the elasticity of taut steel
cables pulling me back across. Wet
bitter tears stay wet bitter tears
during such journeys.
                              Pillow damp
against fingers dovetailed behind my head,
thumbs prying my ears skyward, eyes
crusting shut, lips salty, breathing
muffled to an inaudible crawl, I am
lulled this morning by the decibels
of Dad's clock, battery shot, spasmodic
down the long narrow

catacombs of dreams—Dad's clock
thrilled out of sync.
                        A metronome
beckoning in exotic tempos we must hope
someday to jam to, it is the time
of redefining, of learning to rewind
time, of rewriting the word,
every word, each syllable, all riffs,
cover to leather-bound cover. It is
the time of revising both wisdom and myth
of this imperfect earth.
                        Eager to keep
time with our curious new music
bootlegged through the labyrinthine
waterways, out of the artesian
wellspring of tears
and into the here-and-now, we,
eventually dwelling in the crystalline abyss
of our own presence, become time. It
is only then that we will begin
to tick within the mystical
twistings—oh, will we ever tick—
so deep, all of the burled
other worlds, deathfully still, *will* listen.

Aces and Eights

They say Kesey's dead
but never trust a Prankster
even underground
       Wavy Gravy haiku
      Rolling Stone

When I declare my game—when I hammer
home hard in this here poem
how I absolutely refuse to deal
life's most glaring imperfection, *death*—
people, in religious dance-troupe sync,
stepping one giant step
back from the green circular felt,
gaze at me like I'm playing
with a factory-defect deck, like I'm two
tacos shy of the super-combo plate. You bet,
I tell them, Elvis lives. Kesey, I say,
joining Houdini, Garcia, Leary, trust me,
continues to prove further
the universe truly is God's best
magic-trick acid-trip flick
captured in 6-D
on the mother of all real
big silver screens. Part illusion,
part hallucination, part very blue

humor—kind of your tie-dyed hybrid cross
between *trompe l'oeil* and mirage—we,
skipping our own funerals, hating to miss
those hilarious standup eulogy bits,
rotate to the next table
where, yet again, and don't say I didn't tell you
so, *death* just isn't in the cards.

For Ed McClanahan and Gordon Stevens

How Near Viet Nam Came to US

The I.D. bracelet I never did give
my first girlfriend cost me more
than I'd ever spent before on love
of anything but beer. We sipped
cherry cokes to nickel-a-hit
Rolling Stones' "Let's Spend the Night
Together," "Paint it Black," "Time
Is on My Side," and "I Can't Get No
Satisfaction." I wanted her eyes gleaming
my gold surprise—one small touch
from diamond—something to sanctify
going all the way, something I hoped
would stave off the ultimate pain
all love comes to
without warning. We both went cold
against the mix of malt shop rollick,
the carhop motioning her
to the telephone news from a TV war
forced home too real—everything
in our teenage, red-Chev niche
eclipsed by this foreign dark:
an eight-day fire fight,
some napalmed hill of jungle

dubbed in numbers, her cousin
tallied to the M.I.A. His name
stamped in cheap metal
meant more than all
the Earth's romantic verse
of rock-and-roll inscribed in gold,
more than any purple-hearted Requiem
a red, white, and blue
united world or I could ever give.

Red Light

Revved-up on lust in the crosswalk
two fledgling teens, holding hands,
flaunt, preen, promenade, strut
their youth with cock-a-doodle-doo pomp
just one vintage Chevrolet hood's length away
from me—in my fifties, of the sixties—caught
somewhere between sock hops and Woodstock,
between Viet Nam and Iraq
in this stoplight time warp, radio
tuned to the oldies station—*shaboom-*
shaboom to "Tombstone Blues"
to *let it be, let it be,* so loud
these lovebirds, joined at the thigh,
glance my way. Never before have they
been lit into flames by such
a large scarlet car, vermilion paint
framed in polished chrome, front bumper
distorting their oneness of love
like a funhouse mirror.
                              I strain
my hippest black-cowboy-hatted-
in-lieu-of-full-head-of-hair-
over salt-'n'-pepper mustached
grin, flex my sinew, my buff
forearm out the window like a buzzard wing,

drape my right bicep
oh-so-bitchin' and groovy
man...I mean "dude"...
over the seatback. All this pose
lacks is a pack of Luckys,
a lariat-loop slow motion smoke ring
floating into some thick noir
plot, the moody James Dean, young
Brando or Newman sitting in for me
as a body double.
          The couple, in unison,
smiles—teeth brighter than simonized chrome
over a pair of four-barrel-carb hearts,
skin, tighter, smoother, more gloss
than any new paint job, washed and chamoised,
chatoyant in the noon sun. The girl
lip-syncs two syllables, unfurling, bending
them into a sensual red symphony—"*sweeeet
riiiii-ddde*"—with a slight kiss-
tossing lift of her chin that teases
her onyx-black hair
away from the exact spot
upon her cheek where I fantasize
placing my platonic peck
of pure gratitude.
          Long after
the light turns green, I sit idling

in neutral—beyond lust, beyond
life's rearview noise—yearning only
to soak in this innocence,
meld it with my own
long ago and just yesterday, both
always and never in a simpler time,
a more perfect world, any world
less tormented by war. What I want
desperately to remember of this hopeful
episode is the metaphorical deep pink
double-fisted his-and-her
fingers clenched together, raised
toward me in revolutionary salute, prayer,
praise and mourning to youth, crimson-needled
arc of darling years
punched 0-to-60 in the lurid
blue of far, far, far too few seconds.

In Memory of Carole DeMarinis

Snapshot Gravity

Sacramento. Outer city. Mid-autumn
Saturday morning. Mid-sidewalk. Pushed
in a wheelchair, the gray-stubbled man,
dapper in his red plaid
tam-o'-shanter and matching lap robe,
comes grizzled face to grizzled muzzle
with a swaybacked gimpy Saint
Bernard-Rottweiler-maybe-Lab cross
pushed on a limp leash. Traffic jammed,
frantic, we—two anxious friends
lamenting with country-western threnody
the body's plummeting descent—catch
between snatches of the oncoming
cars, the shutter-quick
glimpse of this soft
jowl-to-cheek encounter. The old
dog licks the elderly man's sad face
into hysterics, into a laughter
out of his past. Hands
invisible, arthritic, anchored in his lap,
the man turns the other cheek
for more, their fun-loving nuzzle
facing the busy street
as if posing for the impossible shot. Why not
lift this picture from the fixer
solution in our darkrooms
shingled with 8-by-10 action

glossies of good karma? Why not
paste the captionless snap,
solo and centered, upon the black
last page of the hefty album
gravity will likely someday keep us all
from lifting off the bottom shelf? Time
decides who becomes this earth's most
kindred—family, friends, acquaintances,
giving way to a blood-brotherhood
of strangers. Old man, old dog,
old portrait voyeurs—we all
take our over-exposed strolls
deeper into the residential flesh
where our hearts' silent horns rejoice
after each close call, every chance
collision of reckless love.

For Quinton and Nancy

Watching the Sun Set over Santa Fe—
City of Holy Faith

We could praise this sky with names of fruit—
orange, apricot, plum—paint it ocher, rouge, perse,
call it the palette of Georgia O'Keeffe. We could
liken these textural hues of cumulus
to pink gingham, tamarisk, chamisa, chenille.

But tonight we pay tribute to flesh,
to vascular tissue. We marvel at
the surge of blood cells, microscopic
within sheer capillaries—the undulant
running of the bulls through narrow streets
in Pamplona. We behold the heat and tremor,
how hemoglobin sparks a bonfire of muscle,
how fibers flame to crimson pinnacles, and then
we witness the quick swoop
accelerating toward ash-
drab residue we shudder
to believe is the soul. I stare at you
in desperation, the day's last remnant
dissolving into once-blue irises of your eyes.

If lucky, we'll embrace a lifetime
trilogy of sunsets this vital—if blessed,
a church spire will grace one of those twilights,
and if, on the eve that steeple appears, we harbor
a tint of what's eternal, we'll sail
with someone we'll love beyond youth,
sail by moonless faith until sunrise.

For Elizabeth

Sweet Wicked Sin

No Forbidden Flowers

She turned eighteen high at Woodstock
In 1969
Peace-'n'-love was all
She lived for then
Janis Joplin crying
Crying "Summertime-time-time"
And Joe Cocker getting by
With just a little help from friends.

She turned thirty-three in chemo
Another goddamn war
Rock-'n'-roll and roll
A joint for pain
Looking back on Woodstock
How it poured and poured and poured
She's so glad she saved that snapshot
Of her topless in the rain.

> No forbidden flowers
> Amidst her hollyhocks
> Just music's magic powers
> Where the doves outlast the hawks
> No more hidden flowers
> No calendars or clocks
> Cuz time is just illusion
> An hourglass of rocks.

She turned fifty in her garden
The new millennium
They said she wouldn't live
Past thirty-five
She blows a kiss to Mother Earth
Blows a smoke ring toward the sun
Takes another toke in Eden
Turns her back on Father Time.

> She's more hopeful every morning
> As she sings to greet the dawn
> Peace-'n'-love is what
> She'd die for now
> No more counting birthdays
> She just lives from song to song
> Letting all the old years go
> Brings the young ones back around.

No forbidden flowers
Amidst her hollyhocks
Just music's magic powers
Where the doves outlive the hawks
No more hidden flowers
No calendars or clocks
Cuz time lost all its powers
When the sand turned back to rocks
Time's only an illusion
An hourglass of rocks.

The Best Dance

(with Betsy Hagar)

In the mirror behind the bar
Between the bourbon and the rye
Her reflection from afar
Will almost make her cry
Every wrinkle, every scar
That her make-up used to hide
She's the girl no one asks
Till the last dance.

With the lights at closing time
Revealing every truth and lie
And each reason with no rhyme
Brings another rude good-bye
It's a shame but not a crime
She no longer wonders why
She's the girl they all leave
With just one dance.

> As she moves, her silhouette
> Becomes a graceful candle flame
> As she sways like Juliet
> To her lover's serenade
> Looking back without regret
> Charms the darkness on its way
> While she dances with the girl
> Who's the best dance.

Though she knows it makes it worse
To tag along with younger friends
Not much blessing, mostly curse
In a world that's all pretend
There are pictures in her purse
Of her lovers way back when
She's the girl they all begged
For the first dance.

Sippin' cognac from a go-cup
While her T-Bird flies her home
Where she will pour a pick-me-up
And her heart into a poem
Getting old means getting tough
So she waltzes all alone
With the girl who knows love
Is a slow dance.

As she moves, her silhouette
Becomes a graceful candle flame
As she sways like Juliet
To her lover's serenade
Looking back without regret
Charms the darkness on its way
While she dances with the girl
Who's the best dance.

She'll always be the girl
Who's the best dance.

The Christmas Saguaro Soiree

(with Betsy Hagar)

She decorates the cactus
The way Great Grandma did
This past year it grew
Another arm or two
She sips some warm mescal
From a tiny Hopi bowl
In the moonlight the saguaro
Shines bright blue.

It's storming in Montana
Where her lover rides
That blue norther doesn't know
It's Christmas Eve
Not feeling one bit lonely
She tinsels every spine
Of the one and only sweetheart
Who won't leave.

    The nectar of agave
    Can spark a miracle
    And suddenly all arms begin to sway
    She celebrates God's birthday
    Peace and love on earth
    With a waltz at the saguaro soiree.

A joyful coyote carol
Drifts down the old arroyo
The red chili lights are strung out
Just like notes
Another sip of mescal
And then she'll raise the angel
First she danced around that cactus
Now she floats.

        The magic land of cactus
        Will soothe her broken heart
        May the icy snowdrifts
        Do the same for him
        From rimrock to adobe
        The Guadalupe sings
        "Tis the season we should wish
        Good will toward men."

The nectar of agave
Can spark a miracle
And suddenly all arms begin to sway
She celebrates God's birthday
Peace and love on earth
With a waltz at the saguaro soiree.

She's dancing with the old ones
Romancing with the earth
In the arms of the saguaro soiree.

Wicked Kiss

(with Wylie Gustafson)

The wicked kiss of sweet tequila
Oh what cards the dark will deal ya
Shady Lady, Ace of Spades
You'll face your demons unafraid.

A shot glass is your crystal ball
Your blue agave waterfall
Your future's pure euphoria
Where your lover meets your warrior.

      Uno mas, Dos Equis back
      Agave gods are keeping track
      One more romance, one more round
      To all the hearts in lost-'n'-found

      Set 'em up and knock 'em down.

The wicked kiss of sweet tequila
Taste the blood of Pancho Villa
Revolutionary juice
Fight for beauty, die for truth.

A shot glass is your crystal ball
A kaleidoscopic free-for-all
Into the *reposado* zone
With Don Julio and Ol' Patron.

Uno mas, Dos Equis back
Agave gods are keeping track
One more romance, one more round
To all the hearts in lost-'n'-found

Set 'em up and knock 'em down...

      Down into the sweet abyss
      Of one more wicked wicked kiss.

The wicked kiss of sweet tequila
Oh what cards the dark will deal ya
Shady Lady, Ace of Spades
You'll face your demons unafraid.

      Uno mas, Dos Equis back
      Agave gods are keeping track
      One more romance, one more round
      To all the hearts in lost-'n'-found

One more reposado down
One more reposado down
Yeah, set 'em up and knock 'em down.

For Bob and Marianne Kapoun

Hope Chest

(with Betsy Hagar)

Hauled her hope chest to a rental shed
Failed marriage memories
Paid the rent up 'til forever
Threw away the padlock keys
Bought a Chev Apache pickup
Like her Daddy used to drive
"She needs some work," the salesman said
"That makes two of us," she sighed.

Found her peace out on the desert
Where nothing ever rusts
Behind her thick adobe walls
Slowly rediscovered trust
She met a man while hiking
He's not the answer, he's the prayer
He knows so much about the stars
She believes he's traveled there.

> Old hope chest in a rental shed
> Beneath thirty years of stuff
> Bedroom sets so sadly stacked
> Heavy residues of love
> Her new hope chest is the desert
> Where she drinks rain without a cup
> Where there's no time for looking back
> She's way too busy looking up.

There's no need for sending flowers
He just delivers her to them
She's his ocotillo blossom
He's her star-of-Bethlehem
They love among the petroglyphs
To the songs of long ago
Kachinas dancing up a storm
To a tears-of-life rainbow.

In her will, whoever reads it
There's a reference to that shed
Jam-packed from floor to ceiling
With remains of love long dead
"Hold the mother of all rummage sales
Sell whatever for a song"
This little bit of letting go
Brought a lot of living on.

> Old hope chest in a rental shed
> Beneath thirty years of stuff
> Bedroom sets so sadly stacked
> Heavy residues of love
> Her new hope chest is the desert
> Where she drinks rain without a cup
> Where there's no time for looking back
> She's way too busy looking up.
>
> Where there's no time for looking back
> She's way too busy looking up.

The Mistress, the Maestro

(with Wylie Gustafson)

Men bleed in the brambles behind wrought iron fences
Surrounding her house in the magnolia trees
Through the black window screens of her candlelit bedroom
The nocturnes she plays drops the wolves to their knees.

In a séance of ivories, of the strings and the winds
The most musical souls, from Mozart to Miles
Some say she seduces her demigod muses
With her dark lingerie and her Gothica smiles.

    She's the mistress, she's the maestro
    Don't I know, oh don't I know

        She's the high wire Bird of the swing saxophone
        The haunting long howl of the Hendrix guitar
        The flaming arpeggio of Chopin's piano
        She's the mistress, the maestro, of *e-rotica*.

Men say she's immortal, born in a horse stall
Long-legged and ebony, with sorrel-red dreads
To church bells and bugles through a thick bayou fog
She's the hot-blooded gallop of a black thoroughbred.

    She's the mistress, she's the maestro
    Don't I know, oh don't I know

She's the phantom of men's fantasies
She's ingénue and she's Medusa
She's the raven organ player
In their loft of gothic dreams.

She is temptress, she is angel
She's Venus and Lolita
Both mythical and real
She is the woman of extremes.

Black widow, black bayou, black snake, black magic
She's the cosmic concoction of a hurricane wind
With her fingernails painted tempestuous purple
Each note she composes is sweet wicked sin.

She's the high wire Bird of the swing saxophone
The haunting long howl of the Hendrix guitar
The flaming arpeggio of Chopin's piano
She's the mistress, the maestro, of *e-rotica*.

She's the mistress, she's the maestro
Don't I know, Lord, don't I know.

Roadwork in the Boneyard

He does his roadwork in the boneyard
Sixty-nine and in his prime
Duckin' the Grim Reaper's hook
Slippin' jabs from Father Time.

He does his roadwork in the boneyard
Shadow boxing his own stone
His epitaph reads, "Do or Die—
Either way, you're on your own."

> You either weaken in your fifties
> As you beg to be excused
> Or order up another round
> As you wine and dine the Muse.

Though he's damn afraid of dying
He's not one bit afraid of death
He likes the coldest darkest nights
Liquid silver in his breath.

He's the maestro of sweet science
He's the Einstein of the ring
But time's no longer relative
With the vultures taking wing.

You either live for the hereafter
Help the churches fill their pews
Or revel in the here-'n'-now
Skipping rope to delta blues.

Rope-a-dope out in the boneyard
Metal fence against his back
He's spitting in the eye of fear
With each lightning flash and crack.

Although death is all around him
He feels closer to his birth
Doing push-ups in the daisies
Stealing kisses from the earth.

You either sink in ol' self-pity
In that cesspool of cheap booze
Or cling to pugilistic youth
With a flurry of one-twos.

Doing roadwork in the bone yard
Shadowboxing your own stone...

Doing roadwork in the boneyard
Toe-to-toe with the unknown.

For Skip Avansino and Joe Brown

5 Memoir Rounds with 1 Paul
Zarzyski:

A Self-Interview

Introduction

Paul Zarzyski works in a twelve-by-twelve room at a desk adjacent to a window facing west, two large aspens mostly blocking his summer view but contributing symphonies of birdsong to his mornings of musical work. At least six horn-of-plenty bookshelves spill out into heaps and stacks of volumes on the 1970s green shag and, out further yet, onto a heavy, light-brown throw rug adorned with dark-brown cattle brands—one of numerous carpet remnants Paul *acquired* while spending a night at the famous Dude Rancher Inn in Billings years ago during the motel's floor renovation. Above the bookshelves, the walls are shingled with original paintings—Larry Pirnie, Walter Piehl, Elizabeth Dear, Sally Brock, Greg Keeler, Tessa Johnson, Theodore Waddell, Tom Russell, and more—original photographs—Jay Dusard, Barbara Van Cleve, Kevin Martini-Fuller, Sue Rosoff, et al.—Jim McCormick-illustrated broadsides of poems, eight-by-ten glossies of Paul riding (at least for one camera-click instant) bareback broncs, and rack after sculpted Ornowood pictorial display rack draped with dozens—make that *hundreds*—of vintage neckties of every motif imaginable, from bucking horse twisters to surrealistic Salvador Dalis to full-frontal cowgirl nudes. Paul refers to the collection as his 401-K. On a more poetic note, he says he loves sporting, "snubbed-up short in a half Windsor over his brisket on stage," the ties he *knows* some old cowboy wore decades back—loves the notion of the cravat still echoing that cowpuncher's or roughstocker's heartbeat and spirit just inches away from Paul's own Rodeo Poet throbbings. I scan the room crammed, layered, bursting with memorabilia, and think to myself, "This is akin to a fool's gold cowboy King Tut's tomb. This space would trigger an anxiety attack in a *Feng Shui* master. This guy Zarzyski gives the term 'pack rat' a bad name!" We're talking 1950s cowboy-'n'-Indian kitsch, snapshots of friends, the quick and the dead—Hugo, McRae, Russell, Zupan, Shuttleworth, Ramblin' Jack Elliott...as well as cowboy collectibles/kitsch/ tchotchkes stacked, hung, displayed, festooned, cubbyholed, *buried*—yes, indeed, a veritable archeological dig. Including one empty bottle of *Viuda de Sanchez* 100 percent de Agave Azul Tequila Reposado, a keepsake of a hearty night enjoyed with writer friends Rick and Carole DeMarinis. *And* a one-of-a-kind- in-the-whole-wide-world four-by-three-inch, hefty, rectangular belt buckle constructed, *sculpted*, by poet Vince Pedroia from a 1920s Corona typewriter typebars—the round ivory Z key set in its silvery bezel centered like a precious gemstone, or a steam locomotive's headlight. And finally, as the nucleus, the hub, the lodestone, the kernel, the umbilicus, the focal and pivot point, the chakra, the very cynosure of the soul's marrow, sits the beloved, notorious, baby-blue Smith-Corona Silent-Super, his mother's, with which Paul has typed every draft of every poem he's ever written.

Round 1

Why 51?

I was born in 1951 in Hurley, Wisconsin, where, throughout the fifties, sixties, and seventies, a huge billboard adorned the southern entrance to the town—it read, "Where **51** Ends And The Fun Begins." I turned **51** years old *a few* years back and ever since, I seem to notice the number appearing before my eyes beyond what statistical probabilities would dictate. This cued me toward a book concept and title—**51**: 30 Poems, 20 Songs, 1 Self-Interview. Since locking-in on the title, the number **51** has become more and more a daily encounter. I wake up in the middle of the night and I swear it's perpetually 1:**51**, 3:**51**, something **51**. Every other highway mileage sign reads Somewhere **51**. I click the television remote to find out how much time remains in a program I'm watching—yup, **51** minutes. The morning Montana weather report forecasts, in the summer, a nighttime low of **51** or, in mid-winter, wind-chills down to a minus **51**. I check my luggage at the airport and I'm perpetually one pound over the 50-pound limit and have to extract the pair of knee-high lucky Tony Lama performance socks and stuff one into each coat pocket. I drive through a 30 mph residential area where they post those flashing digital speed limit warning gizmos and without fail I'm doing **51**. I buy the latest Cross Canadian Ragweed CD, *Happiness and All Other Things*, and the lead-off song, which absolutely rocks, is called "51 Pieces (on the side of the road)." Not to even mention Area 51, which some might say is metaphorically in sync with my temperament. Or the most famous fountain pen ever made, the Parker 51. Or, when touring the Bulleit Bourbon Distillery in Lexington, Kentucky years ago, how the guide emphatically pronounced "at least 51 percent corn" the mandatory requirement for legitimate bourbon whiskies—akin to the 51 percent juice requirement from the spiky leaf agave before our beloved gizzard elixir of the cactus can be dubbed "tequila." And then there's jersey number 51, worn by iconic linebacker Dick Butkus, often deemed "possessed" by his gridiron opponents, even though 51 just so happens to be "the anti-devil number." Moreover, four hundred and 51 degrees Fahrenheit is the ignition temperature of paper, a temperature some readers, in the midst of enduring this long litany of 51 significances, might actually wish for? I'd like to conclude, therefore, with an anecdote that I think will convince them otherwise.

When my muse screams, I click my heels, salute, and heed her desires. Thus, as I prepared to spread my dad's ashes among his twenty-acre woodlot, She beckoned me to dust the bases of 51 of the grandest maples, ash, and oaks. Dad and his good friend Harry cooked moonshine together back in the fifties. I discovered a cobwebbed gallon of the barrel-aged nectar marked *Special* in Dad's hand on the white lid and dribbled a few drops alongside the gray remains beneath each tree. "One for you, Dad, and one for me," I *prayed* with each consecration. I'd take a sip, then stagger to the next hardwood. Somewhere around tree number twenty-three or twenty-nine or thirty-two, I was so impressed by the girth and sculptedness of the trunk that I tipped my head back and stared straight up into the canopy. Fell over backwards, laid there grinning for a spell, then resumed the mission to achieve my Communion of the 51. It had been almost a year since Dad's death, almost two years since learning of his terminal illness. The most difficult time of my life. I sat in his 1967 International pick-up truck for a long while after spreading his ashes. When my head began to clear, I felt an incredible wave of solace. Dad's spirit will thrive in that glorious canopy of 51. He loved mushrooms, and at the base of one of the majestic oaks, stood—yes, *stood*, on its six-inch-diameter stalk—the most ornate toadstool I'd ever seen, its rouged scalloped cap making it look more like a tropical mollusk Dad might've encountered on shore leave than a north woods fungus. I anointed it, as well, with ashes and a splash of hooch. The moment felt so perfect—Dad's final wishes heeded to a tee, thanks in some part, I'm convinced, to the numerological role played by **51**. I don't know—you tell me?

You've written dozens of poems about your dad and your mother. Most speak to your pastoral and passionate upbringing. Tell us about your childhood, the pre-poetry years, which most definitively left an indelible mark on your work.

Anyone who's read the opening essay and poems in my chapbook *Blue-Collar Light* will know what a poetically fertile, sensuous childhood I reveled in—the sounds, the smells, the visuals. Dad worked the iron ore mines while Mom cooked and kept house and tended to the unending needs, to the well-being, of me and my younger brothers, Mark and Gary. I don't remember the shortage of money, although I'm sure it was a daily concern, as much as I recall the abundances of food. I've not yet visited Mom's *old country*, Italy, but I've lived its traditions and ate its cuisine throughout the first eighteen years of my life. And I've heard its dialects spoken daily. My *noni*, my Italian grandmother, lived next door. She cooked on a wood stove and always kept a few cats in the house. I loved staying with her, and though she didn't speak a word of English we didn't have one bit of trouble communicating. "*Noni*," I'd say, "*mi voi pan e caffé*." She'd pour scalding coffee into an ironstone bowl, a *scudella*, and top it off with the cream floating above the milk. Then she'd chop, not slice, because it was stovewood-hard, a chunk of Italian bread off the end of the loaf, my favorite part, and I'd dunk it until soft in the coffee and eat like a lumberjack after a long hard day in the woods. Whoever said, "Man does not live on bread alone," never saw what I mostly lived on for the first ten years of my life. "*Che bello mio Paolo*," *Noni* would praise me, because I didn't ask for meat or cheese, which she could little afford. It pleased her that I was content to eat peasant food. I can brag that I've never been a finicky eater. Even as a kid I savored polenta and veal kidney gravy, liver and onions, stump mushrooms, all vegetables, you name it. And to this day fussy eaters annoy me; in fact, I deem it a serious character flaw. The Food Channel should book *me* as a judge on Iron Chef America. Anyway, I still have my *noni's* ironstone bowl. And to continue to address your question about my 1950s and 1960s upbringing in blue-collar northern Wisconsin, most everyone grew immense gardens and canned, or preserved, until their cellars were full. Most everyone hunted, fished, picked wild berries, hazelnuts, mushrooms. And made salami, *salamini*, kielbasa, much of it out of venison. And pressed wine and distilled grappa, or whiskey. I remember home-brewed root beer, homemade sauerkraut, pickled fish, plums soaked in moonshine, smoked lake trout and canned Coho salmon from Lake Superior. Most everyone *made* wood—heated their homes with wood-burning furnaces in their basements. I can't fathom how the grocery stores stayed in business—flour, sugar, milk, coffee, the basic staples, I suppose. Folks celebrated, boasted about, their subsistence as if it were equivalent to six-figure incomes. Folks worked hard and played hard and talked boldly—because they goddamn *were* bold. Robust, by God. I remember my dad coming home from a shift or double shift underground. First thing he'd do is pour a coffee royal—black java spiked with a hearty splash of moonshine and two to three teaspoonfuls of sugar. He'd likely worked the blasting crew. He'd never pull the sugar bowl from the center of the table over to his cup but instead would reach with his long arm and gigantic hand, "shaking," as he was prone to say, "like a dog shittin' razor blades." He'd scoop a heaping spoonful and by the time it traveled the three feet to his coffee cup, half the expensive contents was all over Mom's oilcloth. Just one more minuscule daily act of defiance among the hundreds of defiant acts those first and second generation immigrants exhibited, a defiance that in turn led to the exuberance of taking *acquiescence's*, or *vulnerability's*, ear between their eyeteeth and bringing it to its knees. I reveled in a childhood surrounded by passionate, stalwart, spiritful adults, that's for sure. I learned to work and work hard. In that *Blue-Collar Light* intro I mentioned, I relate how important it was for me as a boy of five or six to show Mom and Dad my willingness to pull my share of the load. Dad would come home from swing shift at midnight and, sore as my back would get and despite the oftentimes wet, cold spring weather, I'd pick night crawlers until his 1957 Buick turned the corner off Fifth Avenue onto Poplar Street. I made sure he'd see my flashlight beaming above the mossy lawns, my three-pound Hills Brothers Coffee tin filled almost to the brim with the slimy, squirming mass of hundreds of "dew worms," as we called them. Every spring Dad would spike a wooden sign to the corner telephone pole: "Nightcrawlers / 10 Cents a Doz. / 505 Poplar St." Which is the title of a poem that speaks to my earliest love for the satisfactions of hard work. I think I wrote the piece in the late seventies, over thirty years ago, and the closing stanza to this day remains one of my fondest poetic renderings:

> I was young and wondered once
> how my father, tunneling,
> felt the struggle of worms and roots
> working through the earth,
> if he knew how much yellow
> onions grew each night
> in his garden, how close to home
> he really was on graveyard
> shift. I stretched out flat, feeling,
> against each rib, the intimate
> ways of earth
> worms in wet grass, the magnetic
> attraction of man to home
> and hell through rich ore. I pressed
> an ear over a wormhole
> and listened to the medley—
> men, machines, blood, worms—all
> the workings of the body, for love
> or money, mineral or liquid, everything
> living off that one heart of earth.

(Long pause) I'm suddenly reminded of Dad, knowing his fishing days were over, asking my brother Gary to turn loose, to empty into the garden, his tubs of dew worms he'd nurtured all winter. Gary's not a fisherman, but he told me how it devastated him emotionally. I likely would have died of heartbreak on the spot. As I was saying, however, I learned early the significance of resilience, and magnanimity, and, you bet, that critical virtue I call defiance. Defy pain, defy injury, defy complacency, conformity, compliance, compromise. Toward the end of his fight, after the doctor informed him that the dialysis was not tempering the amyloidosis shutting down his kidneys, liver, heart, Dad decided to go off the machines, and the Doc gave him "three to five days, max." Dad hung on for over two weeks. His body withered to skin and bone until his immense, blue-collar hands carried the bulk of his weight. Same hands that built a thousand pieces of furniture, including, a few years after my birth, a twin bed and matching dresser with four portside drawers sporting vertically their **P A U L** alphabet-building-block pulls, while to the starboard, a door opening to a mini-armoire or wardrobe, sported the **Z** pull. Same hands that turned a hundred blocks of balsa into a hundred decoys. "Dekes…He etched / and sanded, whittled and rasped / till grain quilled into feather—mallard, / can (canvasback), or scaup…." Same hands that *made* dozens of annual cords of firewood and mined tons of hematite in the Cary a mile underground. Same right hand that snatched me by my ankles, Muhammad Ali-quick, before I hit the pavement head-first as the door I was leaning against on the 1951 Ford pickup flew open during a left turn. Same left hand that scrawled, by the light of a kerosene lamp, decades of letters to me from the shack he dubbed "S E R E N I T Y"—set in the middle of his twenty-acre woodlot where I spread his ashes. Same thick hands that torqued through the pain of trying to run a fish hook out the other side of a finger so he could snip the barb off and spare himself a doctor bill (maybe you know my poem "Cowboys and Indians"). On his deathbed, he never lost the power in his grip. He *did not* "go gentle into that good night." I spent my entire childhood hoping, trying, to become as vigorous, as resolute and resilient, as my parents.

Why self-interview? Why not simply write this as a personal essay, or pure memoir? Isn't this approach, this format, a bit bizarre?

You got it. "Bizarre," indeed—as in BIZARzyski. Not too bizarre, however, for my mentor Richard Hugo who introduced me to the self-interview in his collection of essays, *The Real West Marginal Way.* I don't know where Dick got the idea—maybe from James Dickey—but I loved the playfulness and pointedness of the approach. I mean, who bolder and better-informed to pose the grittiest questions to oneself *than* oneself? To *pose* to oneself as well as, hopefully, *ex*pose oneself? I'll admit, at fifty-nine years of age, I feel more of a willingness, if not a *need,* to reveal facets of myself that the poems and songs, thus far, perhaps have not—to streak, to stand naked philosophically, emotionally, intellectually, spiritually. To come clean. To confess, lest you forget I grew up

Catholic. To bear witness, present my testimony, place my *left* hand upon *The Book According To Zarzyski* and vow to tell the truth, the whole truth, and nothing but the truth, so help me Maestro of the Musical Universe. I've done at least a hundred interviews with writers working for newspapers and magazines, as well as with radio and television hosts. On a good number of those occasions, I'd go away thinking, "That was intense, deep— we most certainly managed to crack through the thick crust of the mundane." And then I'd read or hear or see the edited versions and was always perplexed. Either my most far-reaching responses wound up on the cutting room floor and/or were lost forever in the ether, or else I didn't articulate my thoughts lucidly enough for interviewers to interpret them into a fodder that their readers, listeners, viewers could assimilate. Maybe I had merely rattled off cheap platitudes that I'd delusively mistook for rich profundities, I'd indict myself. So I've been itching to borrow the self-interview concept for the past two decades—to see if I (we!) can get it right, to see if I (we!) can get my most brutally-candid responses into print, for a change, once and for all. I have never in my life been more enamored with the possibilities for an honest, unpulled-punches exchange between the ego and the alter ego, or *alter idem*—between the self and the second self. Between the yin and the yang? Or, as long as we're talking the universe, I'm a Gemini—Castor meets Pollux, twin meets twin. Am I making any sense?

I think so? I'm not sure.

Okay then, how about if I divulge this tactic as simply a lazy man's essay? For me, conversing colloquially—fielding concrete or *tangible* questions articulated on the page—is much easier than addressing meditative questions that must be *intimated* in the white spaces between correlating sentences of congruent paragraphs. I'm a novice prose writer, okay, and as such I choose to believe, true or false, that one does not *read* an interview, but rather *listens* to it. And listeners, I choose again to believe, are less exacting. All this said, I feel compelled to offer a disclaimer based on the response from my dear friend Wallace McRae, who, when I told him about my intentions to interview myself, emphatically said, "Why do you presume that anybody gives a shit about your ideologies, ethics, or philosophies, to begin with?" Wally makes a good point. Other than perhaps a handful of serious fans of my poetry, who is there to care what worldly or, more tenuous yet, otherworldly perceptions and sensibilities make me tick. Especially when we both know up front that *nothing* I convey to you will abolish war and/or ignorance—will result in a humane, civil alternative to killing one another as an acceptable means of settling differences. I, too, am weary of the more-often-than-not inflated image and, therefore, inflated significance of the interviewee. So let's set the record straight right out of the gate. I am *keenly* aware of just how artistically inconsequential is my creative contribution. On this matter, at least, delusional I am not. If for no other reason, solely because I have in my possession a collection of beautifully inscribed—to people who are yet alive and well—poetry books and CDs by that wordsmith extraordinaire, Paul Zarzyski. I've picked these up in thrift stores and at yard sales—none, so far, plucked from the FREE box, I'm relieved to report. Do you see how that's enough in itself to ensure minimal ego-overload?

Yes, I do. But now let's carry on and see if we can't prove your guru friend, McRae, wrong. You studied with Hugo in the seventies. What did you learn from him about ars poetica?

Years ago I wrote a poem titled "Scars Poetica." It was prompted by songwriter Dave Alvin's fine book of poetry, *Any Rough Times Are Now Behind You*. Renowned sports writer Red Smith pronounced, "Writing's easy—just open a vein and let it flow." Yes, and every time you open that vein, it leaves a little scar. Maybe Mr. Smith was paraphrasing the Turkish poet Nazim Hikmet, who said, "Poetry is the bloodiest of arts—one must offer his heart to others and feed on it himself." I was quoted, and footnoted, by my friend Ralph Beer in his novel *The Blind Corral* as saying, "If there's not at least a little bit of hurt in your life every day, then you're not living hard enough." That dictum was easier to fulfill back in the days when I was riding bucking horses. On second thought, maybe it's a lot easier to subscribe to today when my focus is almost purely on writing rather than divided between the riding and the writing, the latter, of course, the more arduous of the two contact art forms. In any case, that poetry is all about pathos and pleasure, music and message—as well as the infinite extensions therefrom—is the colossal lesson I learned from Dick Hugo. I'm convinced that no other creative writing teacher could have conveyed those poetic essences to me, at that moment of my greenhorn life, as demonstratively as Hugo did.

One spring the two of us decided way too prematurely to fish Twin Lake up in the Mission Mountains. The road, with its twenty inches or so of heavy, wet snow, was damn near impassable. I chained-up all four wheels on the Ford and somehow we managed to claw and buck our way in, only to find merely a trickle of open tributary water and the lake capped in honeycombed ice, which did not deter us from spud-barring a number of holes and completing our mission to wet our lines. At one particularly hairy moment on the ride in, I remember Dick, chain-smoking times three his usual nicotine intake, proclaiming how at ease he felt with me at the wheel. We were miles from the pavement, it was impossible to turn the truck around on such a narrow road, and I didn't have the heart to say, "Dick, our chances of making it in or having to walk out are fifty-fifty." Apply this scenario metaphorically to the classroom and reverse the roles, and you'll know exactly how *I* felt sitting shotgun next to Hugo in the writing workshops. As self-effacing as Dick so often came across, he was nothing less than a literary genius, a brilliant teacher—incapable of putting flimsy thinking or grooveless music into words. Read his poetry. Read *The Triggering Town* and *The Real West Marginal Way*. I doubt I'll be able to summon up even a tenth as much puissance as Richard Hugo evoked via his bouquet of sharpened number 2 pencils sticking out of their Chinook Salmon-labeled tin can vase. Nevertheless, I'm the most fortunate uneducated aspiring writer to have ever entered an MFA program, period.

"Uneducated?"

In a literary sense, unpracticed, unequipped, unprepared, uninformed, uneverything literary. Or to couch it cowboy-colloquially, à la my friend Wylie Gustafson, "dumber than a hundred head of sheep." At twenty-two years old I'd written less than a dozen poems and probably had read less than a few dozen significant books when I strolled into my first workshop at the University of Montana in the fall of 1973. I discovered within minutes that I—compared to my fellow students—was attempting to become the first *poetic pitcher* ever to make the leap from peewee league to the majors. I'd spent my first eighteen years in essentially a bookless house; we watched television. To this day I owe a debt of gratitude for passing grades in English classes to the inventor of *Cliffs Notes*. At the same time, I had a knack for conveying ideas and emotions onto the page via musical sentences. And moreover, I looked, I listened, and I pondered what I saw and heard. Wrote a poem in the early nineties called "Words Growing Wild in the Woods." I think it indirectly speaks to my having taken a shine at a very early age to the vernacular, jargon, patois, slang, colloquialisms, idioms, locutions of blue-collar, small-town, ethnic America, much of its lingo rooted in nature's lexicons. Never thought of it as the makings of poetry. Further yet from my cognizance, I certainly couldn't have recognized its kinship back then to cowboy lingo, which, how could I ever have guessed, would someday become such a significant facet of my writing. Yes, "uneducated" in any kind of a formal sense, no doubt, but looking back now, I'd have to say that I was hanging around poetry for two decades prior to choreographing works into a form that I loosely referred to as "poems." Oh, before I forget, a brief postscript to this response: Hugo wrote a recommendation, after I graduated in the mid-seventies, in which he informs prospective employers that it is not ignorance but ethnicity behind my pronouncing *ths* like *ds*. It's probably still in my reference file at the University of Montana. And *dat's* my last word on *da* matter.

So what you're intimating is that you deem yourself the most improbable poster child for the vocation of poetry?

Not to fly off the sesquipedalian alliterative handle on you, brother, but my proletarian upbringing bucked all prosopographical poetry postulations. At twenty years of age, the *last* passion I thought I'd ever pursue was poetry. From a distance, blue-collar audiences think I write the way I do because of formal training. On the contrary, it was *in*formal observation that informed whatever foundation as a writer I aimlessly constructed for myself. Dick Hugo reinforced my inkling that I possessed both the tympanum and the ticker to write meaningful, musical poetry, and after that it was simply for me a matter of incurring more and more joy, revel, satisfaction, wild-ass highs from the process, the journey. Sam Shepard once referred to the writing endeavor as a "maladjustment;" I believe Tom McGuane spoke of it as "anti-life" in an early essay. For me it's an addiction. Maybe not cocaine or booze, but easily caffeine. My mother confessed recently that as an infant I took to coffee like a Labrador pup takes to a city park duck pond. She said she finally just put a little in my baby bottle. Also rubbed moonshine on my gums to ease the teething—ahh, *those* were the days 'ey? Little could Mom have known that she, via caffeine fixes, via her symphonic Italian lilts and her incredible penchant for sentimentality, was inflicting, or I should say *bestowing*, upon me a poetry addiction. I got the bucking horse, the physical, the adrenaline-fueled vigor from my dad—though, again, he too instilled, as Hugo referenced it *ad infinitum*, "love for the sound of words," for "Words Growing Wild in the Woods."

A boy thrilled with his first horse,
I climbed aboard my father hunkering in hip boots
below the graveled road berm, Cominski Crick
funneling to a rusty culvert. Hooking
an arm behind one of my knees, he lifted
with a grunt and laugh, his creel harness creaking,
splitshot clattering in our bait boxes.

I dreamed a Robin Hood-Paladin-Sinbad life
from those shoulders. His jugular pulse rumbled
into the riffle of my pulse, my thin wrists
against his Adam's apple—a whiskered knuckle
prickly as cucumbers in our garden
where I picked nightcrawlers, wet and moonlit,
glistening between vines across the black soil.

Eye-level with an array of flies, every crayon
color fastened to the silk band
of his tattered fedora, the hat my mother vowed
a thousand times to burn, I learned to love
the sound of words in the woods—Jock Scott,
Silver Doctor, Mickey Finn, Quill Gordon, Gray
Ghost booming in his voice through the spruce.

At five, my life rhymed with first flights
bursting into birdsong. I loved
the piquant smell of fiddleheads and trilliums,

hickory and maple leaf humus, the petite
bouquets of arbutus we picked for Mom.
I loved the power of my father's stride
thigh-deep against the surge of dark swirls.

Perched offshore on boulder—safe from wanderlust
but not from currents coiling below—
I prayed to the apostles for a ten-pounder
to test the steel of my telescopic pole,
while Dad, working the water upstream and down,
stayed always in earshot—alert and calling to me
after each beaver splash between us.

I still go home to relearn my first love for words
echoing through those woods: *I caught one!*
Dad! I caught one! Dad! Dad!
skipping like thin flat stones down the crick—
and him galloping through popples, splitshot ticking,
to find me leaping for a fingerling, my first
brookie twirling from a willow like a jewel.

*So a poem in praise of your dad's penchant for words is fueled by
your mom's sentimentality. But isn't sentimentality considered a
literary fault?*

Fitzgerald said, "The sentimental person thinks things will
last—the romantic person has a desperate confidence that they
won't." I'm a hybrid-cross, I suppose—a sentimental romantic?
Or maybe *I'm* a "literary fault"? To answer your question, not
according to Bill Kittredge and Hugo, it's not. Both professed in
the Montana classroom what is rumored to be a proverb that
poet Gary Thompson relayed from the California classroom: "If
you're not risking sentimentality, you're not even in the ballpark."
You bet, the key word is "risk"—a tiptoed, lean-out-over, not a
belly-flop-into, the blue saccharine pool of maudlin or mawkish
Hallmark card goo. And speaking of risk, in a flashback to my
invoking Sam Shepard's name, I once heard an interviewed friend
of his say, "The thing about Sam is he has always been willing to
fail but fail interestingly, and if you're willing to fail interestingly,
you'll succeed." So much of what we do as artists fulcrums off our
willingness, or lack thereof, to stretch—to "reach!" as the old jazz

musicians shouted to a fellow player running with a riff—to test the edges, to walk the Philippe Petit high wire between towers. The 4-F *affirm*-ment, not *defer*ment, I like to call it, echoing off the old conscription era draft status and transmogrifying it into something all poets, all artists, should aspire to in approaching the creative process—Freedom, Fearlessness, *Fierceness*, Fun. To put it in roughstock-twister-ese, "take that extra tuck and let the lingo buck!" Did you come to hide? Or did you come to ride? To spur the words wild? Nets, roll bars, seat belts, helmets, bullet-proof vests, panoplies, bear bells, shark repellent, sun screen, safety glasses, rain gear, mosquito dope, ginko biloba boluses not encouraged.

Fierceness?

Plucked it years ago from Gretel Ehrlich's *The Solace of Open Spaces*: "To be tough is to be fragile; to be tender is to be truly fierce."

Lovely.

If you see her before I do, mention *our* fondness and gratitude, will you?

I'll likely cross paths with Gretel before I will with high-wire artist, Philippe Petit. Philippe Petit? I must admit surprise. You've seen his documentary, Man On Wire, *I take it?*

Yes, ten or fifteen years *after* I read, again and again, Petit's book, *On The High Wire*, thanks to Teresa Jordan, who introduced me to it, and thanks to Anne Widmark, who gave me a personal copy of the book. Here's Annie's letter, dated November 9, 1999, inside the front cover: "Hey Paulski, I finally found Petit! Someone told me that he's artist in residence at The Cathedral of St. John the Divine, so I put 2 + 2 together and *voila!*" I seem to recall Teresa saying that she interviewed Philippe for some newspaper or magazine. In any case, she figured correctly that I'd recognize a strong kinship between Petit's passion and that of the poet. My years of holding down so-called "visiting lecturer" teaching positions were forever behind me, or else I'd have assigned *On*

The High Wire as the required *poetry* text for every class I taught. Let me read several highlighted passages:

> Attention! You own the wire, that's true. But the essential thing is to etch movements in the sky, movements so still they leave no trace. The essential thing is simplicity. That is why the long path to perfection is horizontal.

Is not the poet's "long path to perfection" the *stich*, the line? Especially, perhaps, the first and (sometimes far more challenging) the last line? All that wonder-filled, miraculous, dazzling height and quintessential defiance *of* —and, in the same breath, camaraderie and collaboration *with*— gravity? Listen further:

> ...he stands before the cable, as if he did not dare set foot on it. He measures space, feels out the void, weighs distances, watches over the state of things, takes in the position of each object around him. Trembling, he savors his solitude....Alone on the wire, he wraps himself more deeply in a wild and scathing happiness, crossing helter-skelter into the dampness of the evening...he goes out on his wire with only one goal: to discover new ideas, to invent a combination of unexpected gestures. He goes out hunting. And what he catches he hangs on his wire....It is the wire that links the finite to the infinite: the straightest, shortest path between one star and the next....The wire trembles. The tendency is to want to calm it by force. In fact, you must move with grace and suppleness to avoid disturbing the song of the cable.

"The song of the cable"! Is this not a poet traversing the poetic wire? One more, and then we'll move on. From "The Wire Walker at Rest." I'd like to read you the whole chapter, but....

> Keep going until you reach the other side of the light. It is a dazzling clarity, a clamorous splendor: wet, whirling, often colorless. As if through a black mirror, you will see a gleaming, untouched

wire. That is the image you are looking for. It will quickly be jumbled together with the fireworks of new impressions. Once this image has come, however, the high wire walker can live in space. For whole hours, for portions of entire days, as if time had come to a halt.

That's *it!* The eureka moment! *That's* how I feel in the middle of a line in the middle of a high wire writing shift. The poet as funambulist! That's *it!* And then there's the film you mentioned, with its definitive metaphor conveying the epicenter of The Creative Endeavor—Petit, with one foot already out on the cable, lifting, heel to ball to big toe, the other foot up and off the Trade Tower's ledge and out, through thick air, into and onto the unknown. Liz and I and, how fitting, Annie Widmark, first saw *Man On Wire* in a small theater in Santa Fe—maybe twenty people in the audience. I clung often to the seat in front of me. And when he took that second step out between the towers, I wept, I *wept*—I wept with revelation, I tell you. Ever since that moment, I've deplored, more than ever, artistic complacency—playing it safe for the sake of, I think, in most cases, your audience. I didn't notice the thousands of onlookers, as Petit traversed, eight— yes, 8—magical times, the void between the Towers...I didn't notice them rushing to string netting beneath him, did you? As an artist, you best learn—the earlier, the better, in your creative life—to adopt a "love-'em-'n'-leave-'em, catch-'n'-release" relationship with your audience. The applause seldom comes without payback, without future expectations on their part. The applause empowers your audience to dictate, if you allow them to, more of the same from you, more of what they've applauded in the first place. When I ponder the antithesis or flip-side to this syndrome, I flash repeatedly to Bob Dylan. Arguably, no artist of *our* generation allotted less power to his audience. (Photographer Robert Mapplethorpe, maybe.) We're talking Fearlessness and Freedom to the umpteenth power of F squared. The opening lines of my lyric, "Roadwork in the Boneyard," read: "He does his roadwork in the boneyard / Shadowboxing his own stone / His epitaph reads *Do Or Die / Either way, you're on your own.*" I rest my case about pandering to audience.

What changes if Philippe Petit had fallen to his death?

Good question. In my view, not much changes beyond the ending of the film. Even if the film doesn't get made, the attempt is still documented in the cosmic dust of all creativity. When Petit talks of the possibility of falling, he talks somewhat nonchalantly of "falling to another life." He says, "What a beautiful death— to die in the exercise of your passion." Poet Theodore Roethke proclaimed in his journals, "To write poetry you have to be prepared to die." I love the commentary with which Petit closes *Man On Wire*: "To me, it's simple—life should be lived on the edge of life. You have to exercise rebellion—to refuse your own success, to refuse to taper yourself to rules, to refuse to repeat yourself." I'm not at all perplexed by my poetic affinity for Petit's philosophy to approach life as a work of constantly evolving art, but I am surprised by my fascination with his particular passion. It must have to do with some "attraction to the unfathomable," a phenomenon or principle no doubt defined by psychologists? I mean, you're talking to someone afflicted with serious acrophobia—so afraid of heights I had to abandon my dreams of becoming a rodeo announcer rather than a bucking horse rider because announcers work twenty-thirty feet up in those crow's nests. Seriously, I could far more easily see myself as a sumo wrestler than a tightrope walker.

Or perhaps a prize fighter? You've effected boxing focal points and/or metaphors in a number of your poems and lyrics, including the "Roadwork in the Boneyard" piece, from which you just read. Have you spent time in the ring?

A bunch of rings, but none of them a boxing ring. At least not in this life—so far. As a young boy I watched the Gillette Friday Night fights with Dad. Later I became a Muhammad Ali fan—to this day, he remains one of my heroes. I stand up and salute every time I'm reminded of what he said as part of his reasoning for refusing to be drafted—"No Vietnamese ever called me 'nigger'." I love Tom Russell's song, "Muhammed Ali," love the documentary film *When We Were Kings*. I've hung a heavy bag in the basement or garage of every place I've lived since moving to Montana in seventy-three. For cardiovascular purposes—to temper testosterone overloads, to defuse, to

144

prevent appearances of my fucking mushroom cloud rampage aftermaths, to take the edge off my Polish-Eye-talian-UniPoet-Hitman-angst. What can I say? Yoga alone doesn't do it for me. And on the wages of poetry, I can't afford Pilates classes or a Nordic Track. On May 2, 2009, I sat front row, right next to ring announcer Michael Buffer—Jack Nicholson six rows behind me—at the MGM Grand Arena and watched Manny Pacquiao knock out Ricky Hatton in two action-packed rounds. Thanks to my friends Skip Avansino and Joe Brown—current and former Nevada State Boxing Commissioners, respectively—who became fans of my work at the Elko Cowboy Poetry Gathering. I don't know if I need, or want, to defend my affection for such a brutal sport, other than to say I lean toward one-on-one competitions—writer against the blank page. And trust me, it will buck you off. It will counterpunch. It will bloody your nose and knock you on your ass and kick you in both the head *and* the heart. However, I'm fond of the phrase, of the terminology, employed when one fighter, usually of lesser prowess, is winning on the score cards because "he's outworking his opponent." I like to think of myself as a poet of lesser skills who more often than not "outworks" the blank page. And in the event you forget to pose the standard interview question—*What pursuit or passion would you have chosen had you not been able to choose poetry?*—I'll cover it for you here: In sticking to the letter *p*, I'd have *p*ursued the *p*assions of either the *p*hilosopher, the *p*hilanthropist, the *p*ugilist, the *p*icker (antique or guitar) or the *p*roducer.

Theater? Movie? Music…?

Music—I've come to love the recording studio, thanks to Justin Bishop, to Jim Rooney and Pat Alger, to Gordon Stevens and his cohorts Tim Volpicella, Lee Ray, and Scott Sorkin, to Betsy Hagar and Rich O'Brien, to Wylie Gustafson and John Carter Cash, and others.

A subject I'm hoping to discuss in another round. To punctuate this first round at the closing bell, however, let's try a flurry of axiomatic jabs, uppercuts, combinations. I notice on your book shelf there a line-up of blue National 43-581s (51 with an 8 in the middle)—Dick Hugo's cloth-bound writing notebooks of choice—and I'm hoping you won't mind perusing a few and reading at random favorite maxims, aphorisms, Zarzyski creeds, what have you?

I haven't cracked most of these notebooks in decades. Hard to say what we'll find—certainly not much in the way of profundities from yours truly. Is this what you have in mind?:

> "My language is the universal whore who I have to make into a virgin."
>
> Karl Kraus

> "Whenever you find yourself writing poems you're able to write, stop and reach for poems that are larger than your ability."
>
> John Berryman

Red Shuttleworth takes Berryman's tenet to the next level:

> "There can only be failure when a poet tries to reproduce, replicate, previous success. It's futile to seek past results in new circumstances. I want to change the future...or better, I want to do the literary/poetry impossible: I want to *remember* the future."

Philippe Petit spoke to how most peoples' dreams are tangible, but how his earliest dream of tightrope walking between the twin Trade Towers was "quixotic," as the towers had not yet been designed or built. Maybe this is an example of Red's "remembering the future." Here's a salvo from Theodore Roethke's journals:

> "Bring to poetry the passion that goes into politics or buying a piece of meat."
> "Energy is the soul of poetry. Explosive active language."
> "To make the line in itself interesting, syntactically, that is the problem."

Petit agrees, I'm sure, with Roethke's take on "the line."

146

And now, a pair from Roethke's prize student, Richard Hugo:

> "If what you are doing for a living stops you from writing a poem, you are not a poet."
> "...I don't believe in God. I believe the wind is *like* God, because we can see and feel its effect, but not see *it*."

That one especially rings true for me.

Here then is another that'll likely speak your lingo:

> "God is a comedian playing to an audience who's afraid to laugh."
> Voltaire

And you'll get a kick out of this one, too:

> "A writer can be as emotionally captious as a prom queen wired on meth."
> Jim Harrison

Now that's what I call an original simile.

Oh, yes, from the grande dame, the sister superior, the prima ballerina of our poetry world, Maya Angelou:

> "Music was my refuge. I could crawl into the spaces between the notes and curl my back to loneliness."

I genuflect and bow to her inaugural poem, "On the Pulse of Morning." I actually read a passage from it at the Elko Cowboy Poetry Gathering a few years back. Ahh, here we go—a film fave—from Maya Angelou's contrarian, Robin Weigert, playing Calamity Jane in the HBO series, *Deadwood*:

> "Every day takes figuring out all over again how to fucking live."

You gotta love the poetic syntax of that one. And how could you not shout *bravissimo* to this duet?

> "It is better to die on your feet than to live on your knees."
>
> Emiliano Zapata

> "Freedom is what prohibition ain't."
>
> Merle Haggard

Touché!

And here's one more Hugo-ism I'm fond of:

> "...During the composition of a poem, it is good to know you don't have a friend in the world."

There's Dick's take on that "Caution! Audience Expectation" warning sign I spoke of. Huh! Dig this—captioned, "Zarzyski's birthday boast, May 25, 2004:"

> "My Muse is a nymphomaniac rhythm-'n'-blues singer who owns a liquor store and loves to go fishing."

I guess I was feeling somewhat feisty on the morning of my fifty-third. Here we go:

> "When Jesus said 'Love Your Enemies,' I think He probably meant don't kill them."
>
> Rancho de Taos bumper sticker.

And from Kurt Vonnegut's *Paris Review* Self-Interview:

> "I think it can be tremendously refreshing if a creator of literature has something on his mind other than the history of literature so far. Literature should not disappear up its own asshole, so to speak."

Oh yes, from Jimi Hendrix:

> "When the power of love overcomes the love of power, the world will know peace."

(long pause) **DING!**

I agree—no hitting after the bell.

Round 2

Let's talk for a bit about cowboy poetry and then we'll get back to discussing your serious work.

In the words of Merle Haggard, "You're walkin' on the fightin' side of me."

I apologize. Truth be known, I'm a fan of cowboy poetry. Tell me about your earliest encounters with the cowboy West and, subsequently, with cowboy poetry.

Well it must've all kicked-off with the TV serial westerns and big silver-screen cowboy sagas I watched by the thousands in my childhood. I made my first trip west in 1962 at age eleven, with an uncle, aunt, and cousin, to visit Yellowstone and Glacier Parks. I returned to Montana for a fishing trip with my first girlfriend and her parents some years later, and saw my first rodeo in Townsend. Toss into that slow-but-certain-fermentation-of-a-westerner the 8 mm footage of my dad and his partners hunting mule deer and antelope—of some old cowboy sitting a hammerhead saddle horse and smoking a roll-your-own—around Ekalaka, Montana, and the stage was set for my transplantation. Then the big jump into the rodeo arena, which occurred during my second year in graduate school. My poet compadre—my very first Missoula friend—Quinton Duval, also in the writing program, was a serious aficionado of country-and-western music, C-W in its purest genuine-article, unadulterated, unpasteurized, unpopped-up form—Hank Williams, Jimmie Rogers, Patsy Cline, Lefty Frizzell, Jim Reeves, Rose Maddox, Loretta Lynn, George Jones, Tammy Wynette, you get the picture. We discovered a wonderful band with a lovely and talented female vocalist, Jan Dell, who played five or six nights a week at a honky-tonk called the Cabin in East Missoula. Later they moved to another rough joint, the AmVets Club, a mere serendipitous few blocks from my apartment. You could count on the fingers of a blind butcher's off-cleaver paw the number of nights Quinton and I, during his year in Montana, did *not* take in at least a couple of sets. Hell, eight out of ten nights we—vowing an early departure after just one or two *cocktails*—unwittingly found ourselves experiencing the 1:45 a.m. "last call for alcohol," just as the band broke into their Willie Nelson finale. Let's see if I can recollect a few lines thirty years later:

> Turn out the lights
> The party's over
> They say that all
> Good things must end.
> Call it a night
> The party's over
> But tomorrow starts
> The same old thing again.

Something close to that and, yes, I know, I sing poorly. The band's repertoire was endless and included a half-dozen rodeo songs, including one they called, "Cowboy in a Continental Suit," about a duded-up eastern feller who surprises a bunch of working cowpunchers by fitting a ride to the rankest outlaw in the cavvy, the remuda, the rough string of saddle horses. Found out fifteen years later the song lyric was adapted from an old cowboy poem, "The Zebra Dun," by that prolific old cowboy poet who went by the name of Anonymous. Anyway, I was enchanted by the song, the story—related to it, or maybe aspired to become the protagonist. I borrowed a gut-string guitar and taught myself a few chords. Quinton played pretty well and charted for me the chord progressions to a few Hank Williams hits. A while back I came across an old grad-school folder with Xeroxes of a dozen cowboy songs as well as a number of poems, complete with rust-red paperclip imprints. I vaguely recall exhuming from the dustiest stacks at the university library a Jack Thorpe songbook and Charles Badger Clark's *Sun And Saddle Leather*. I was a writer of, as you put it, "serious poetry." I certainly could not check those books out—sign my real name to the little cards pocketed inside the back covers. I mean, what if somebody decades later discovered that *the distinguished American poet* Paul Zarzyski was once interested in what the literary establishment considers "doggerel." I'm being facetious, of course. The rare volumes, likely in the archives, were not allowed out of the building. But what an ugly word—doggerel—don't you agree?

Yes, but please continue.

So in the summer of 1974, Jan Dell's cowboy husband, Tom Bryant, helped me get cinched down and shake my face for the chute gate on my first bareback bronc at the Flint Crick Valley Days in Philipsburg. I just now realized it was a sort of revisitation of Hugo's great poem, "Degrees of Gray in Philipsburg." The bronc, I remember as if it were yesterday, was named Sheba, a small palomino mare. The announcer slaughtered my name, except for the *ski*, and some old drunk clinging like Spiderman to the chain-link fence yelled, "Ride 'em, you polack sonofabitch." Sheba twitched me off like a pesky fly on the second jump, stepped on my leg, and I was hooked.

Why the big smile waning to such a deep melancholic pondering? Why so pensive all of a sudden?

I don't know. Those were exciting times. Montana. Hugo. Poetry. Rodeo. Horses. New music, new friends, fresh adventures— journeys into the unknown, the frontier. Too much past tense, I guess. I'll never forget pulling into Missoula in September of 1973. I'd hauled a few belongings out earlier that summer. Rented a basement apartment from a retired school teacher, Sylvia Haight, to whom I dedicated in part my first full book of poems, *The Make-Up of Ice*, eleven years later in 1984. I was still living in that basement, still paying seventy dollars a month, utilities included. I wonder what students are shelling out today? Seventy bucks a month, man—that's what I call freedom. I was making a few winning bronc rides, I was writing a few winning poems, I was winning an occasional daily fishing derby against stiff competition—Dick Hugo. I was crisscrossing the Bob Marshall Wilderness with Ripley Hugo's son, Matthew. I was embraced by herds of great friends, some of them writers: Jim and Lois Welch, Rick and Carole DeMarinis, Dick and Ripley (the Wylie Street Gang), Kim Zupan, Ralph Beer, Ed McClanahan, Larry Levinger, Jimmy Lee Burke, Jim Crumley, Neil McMahon, Bill Kittredge, Annick Smith...a veritable who's who of Missoula gurus. Some were writers while others were riders: Kim (both writer and rider), Joe Podgurski, Curt Stewart, Jake Woirhaye, Wayne Bronson, Lloyd Bermingham, Steve Anders, Tim Tamberg....None of us would ever become champions, but we didn't revel in the gypsy-rogue-rounder adventure of it all any less than the gold-buckle winners, the so-called, "wolves of the world." I think I nailed it— our wild-bunch times together—in my piece, "Long Sagebrush Drives: A Polish-Mafioso-Rodeo-Poet Rap." Or, as I recently intro'd it from the stage of the 1920s, art-deco Fox Theater while performing with Wylie & The Wild West backed by the Spokane Symphony, "Buckin' hoss twister, testosterone-fueled, roughstockaholic jabberwocky rap." **L.S.D.**, indeed, because we were on an adrenaline-endorphin-psycho-dellic high, alright. We were by-god "contenders," à la that famous Marlon *On the Waterfront* Brando line. Contenders—in both the rough riding and rough writing arenas. Jim Crumley and Ralph Beer sat in the grandstand at the Missoula County Fair Rodeo one fall when I spurred a pretty good jump-'n'-kicker to the pay window. Jim was so tickled he gave me two pairs of custom-made boots from Texas that he said didn't fit him just right. Hard to believe Dick, Matt, Welch, Jake Woirhaye, Crumley, Carole DeMarinis, and, most recently, my poetry blood brother Quinton Duval, are gone. I've been crying myself to sleep for weeks thinking about the sweet, creative times Q and I shared in the MFA program in 1973 and 1974. He and Gary Thompson—and Andrew Grossbardt, also long gone—taught me as much as Hugo did about poetic craft. Quinton, poor guy, critiqued every poem I've written in the past thirty-seven-and-a-half years. And, did Carole and Rick *ever* throw the mother of all first-book parties for me after *The Make-Up of Ice* was published. We're talking, "back when writers behaved badly," as Jim Harrison put it pithily at Welch's memorial. Back when notorious novelists, to remain anonymous here, were apt to remove cherished family photos from a host's wall and pull the frames apart to acquire unencumbered panes of glass upon which to cut, with a MasterCard more than likely maxed-out, the long white talc-like spokes.

It had to be Crumley

I'm not saying. Although rumors abound that Rick DeMarinis has in his possession a stash of un-retouched snapshots documenting the events of that bash. At one pivotal point of the occasion, Carole apparently snatched a pint of Everclear away from me and Jim—yes, Crumley, goddamnit—as we were passing it back and forth, tears leaking down our cheeks. What I *do* remember, pretty much solely, is the wild drive to the East Gate liquor store for *resupplies* at 1:30 a.m., just under the closing time wire, in Carole's mother's 1971 Monte Carlo, which I still drive. I remember sailing—yes, "sailing" in that land barge of a car—down Van Buren Street doing Saint-Christopher-only-knows how many miles-per-minute over the speed limit, Rick lounging at the tilted-down wheel, me riding shotgun, and two heavyweight, renowned prose writers filling the back seat and nasally inhaling some non-liquid substance—out of orange-ish, plastic pharmaceutical pill-dispensers, no less—through a straw. The Canadian train event, a decade or so earlier, documented by the film *Festival Express*, had nothing over a Missoula book party, I tell you. Carole fixed me pancakes, bacon, and eggs as the sun came up. I strolled out into the brisk fall air and wondered if my poetry life had peaked, if it would all be downhill from then on. Luckily, it hasn't been.

Let's circle back to cowboy poetry. How long after your P-burg debut bucking horse ride—and I realize I use the word "ride" loosely here—did you write your first rodeo poem?

I think my first poem *about* rodeo was "Zarzyski Meets the Copenhagen Angel." Wait a minute—it's coming back to me. After P-burg, I bucked off in Helmville and Drummond that summer—sprained both wrists on a stout bay horse at the latter. In the fall I met my long-time rodeo partner and, to this day, great friend, Kim Zupan. We became, for a season or two, members of the University of Montana Rodeo Team (in fact, we *were* the team) under the tutelage of one Professor Joel Bernstein, a former rodeo cowboy who vicariously relived and rerode, through us, his roughstock-rounder youth. Joel was tickled plumb-pink to funnel our way whatever monies he could wheedle out of the student activities fund. I could relay a thousand hilarious tales surrounding those times, but they have little to do with writing, and the statute of limitations could very well be seventy-seven instead of seven years regarding some of our exploits. Kim wrote prose—still does. Working on a third novel as we speak. He became both a top-hand bareback rider and a top-hand fiction writer. I crafted "Zarzyski Meets the Copenhagen Angel," having lifted the Zarzyski-persona title from the maestro poet, Paul Zimmer ("Zimmer's Head Thudding Against the Blackboard;" "Zimmer, The Luckless Fisherman, Dreams He Is a Fish;" "Zimmer, Drunk and Alone, Dreaming of Old Football Games"), as well as having filched the "Copenhagen Angel" image from an early Chris LeDoux song. This was in the 1970s, let's not forget, long before the revival or reincarnation of cowboy poetry in 1985 with the first Gathering in Elko.

So you did not refer to the "Copenhagen Angel" piece as a "cowboy poem," per se?

Right. It was after my first Elko go-round in 1987 before I began to think of my work fitting under that label—sporting the CP brand—in large part because of subject matter. To make the designations and definitions all the more convoluted, I've never thought of myself as a cowboy. I've never *cowboyed* for a living. Therefore, *I Am Not A Cowboy*, as declared by the title of the book I choreographed with artist friend Larry Pirnie in 1995. "All hat and no cattle," as the staunchest critics of cowboy poet poseurs enjoy deeming us. During my most successful rodeo seasons, I maybe broke even, if we're just talking prize money that is. In my heyday prime, I was at best an average bronc twister. Factor in the dozens of poems and song lyrics triggered by my rodeo experiences, however, which in turn graced me with entrée to the cowboy stages, and, hell, I can rationalize my rodeo career as a colossal financial success. Far more importantly, I will never forget those wild, split-second moments when, sittin' pretty in the midst of a spur ride, I caught brief but clear glimpses of the old cowboy west, of the whang leather, sand, rawhide, and wild hearts those top-hand men *and women* were concocted from and powered by. And when the big, splayed front hooves of that bronc I was straddled to like a tuning fork hit terra firma, I staked my claim to the music of the West. Moreover, as a fifty-nine-year-old poet whose name has never appeared until just recently on a property deed (my dad left me his twenty-acre woodlot), I by God *owned*, and *still* own, and always *will* own, those eight-to-ten-inch arena hoof-print cores to the molten-depth center of the earth. Yup, you're looking at a real estate magnate, a land baron of western nobility, alright. Thus I prefer the handle *Rodeo* Poet, especially when we're talking my free-verse, jump-'n'-kick lines across the arena or open range of the page. Rodeo Poetry is far more metaphorically and musically accurate—the ring of it, the assonance.

So you wrote Rodeo Poetry for a decade prior to Cowboy Poetry's renaissance, yet you were not invited to the first Elko Gathering because...?

...because, I was told later, my work was not in sync with the genre's traditional rhymed and metered forms.

But certainly you'd written...?

...not much and only when I was *forced* to fulfill assignments for some upper-level prosody class. *Exercises.* Not the free-of-fences, unfettered, un-pilloried poetry I've come to know and love. Frankly, I harbor not a single ambition to become a sequacious mimicker of literature. Charles Bukowski, denouncing the New Formalism, nailed it for me when he said, "As the spirit wanes, the form appears." Thank you, Brother Buke.

Are you sure you want to announce in print your aversion to the masters, the forms into which they crafted their historically significant work?

Again, I've decided it is not so much the young at heart who should represent the virtue of defiance as it is the old at heart—defiance and humility, not mutually exclusive virtues, in my view. I'm way too old to temper and censor my gut responses. To quote African-American poet Lucille Clifton's opening statement to a Nebraska audience decades back, "I'm not here today to comfort the afflicted, but rather to afflict the comfortable." In my head-bowed-humble, blue-collar, enigmatic-maverick-iconoclast opinion, the making of powerful art has a lot more to do with blazing fresh trails into the infinite frontier known as Life Lived to Its Creative Utmost than it does with a pedantic regurgitation, templating, echoing, cloning, plagiarizing and/or paraphrasing of our artistic ancestors. In the same breath, however, only a fool doesn't believe that we and everything we do links up out there in the musical universe—not only connects to, but depends upon, all that precedes us. There's no such thing as cutting the cord, going it alone—no solo-flight accolades or *mea culpas*. Every word ever spoken or written has its nexus to someone or something. This admitted, the making of art, in my view, is nonetheless more about innate, organic, uncalculated, spontaneous responses to *informal living* than it is about so-called *formal schooling*. The longer I write, the less acknowledgment I pay to paradigms and hierarchies; the life and work of, for example, Charles Badger Clark or my contemporary Henry Real Bird is *equal to*—on the same scale of weights and balances—the life and work of William Butler Yeats or William Carlos Williams.

Go on. As long as you've dug yourself in this deep, you may as well keep shoveling.

Our mission—as I see it from my admittedly unusual vantage point—is *not* to delineate, dissect, explicate, define, fence it all off. Remember that marvelous scene in *The Dead Poet's Society*? Robin Williams, playing a prep school English professor, John Keating, instructs his students to rip out a textbook introduction, "Measuring Poetry," because the writer mandated that poetry's worth or merit, "the measure of greatness," be judged on a graph according to subjective criteria. Williams proclaims, "Words and poetry can change the world....We read and write poetry because we are members of the human race, and humans are passionate." I love that scene—*that's* what I call teaching.

Your repertoire, since becoming involved with the cowboy poetry movement in 1987, does, in fact, include a number of rhymed and metered works, most of which address lighter-hearted subject matter. A harsher observer might say "trite" or "corny" subject matter?

By whose standards? As Dick Hugo proclaimed in *his* self-interview, "I'm not ashamed of having corn in my poems. All good art has a measure of schmaltz." Moreover, the *whimsical* or even *quirky* wild rhymers in much of my work became, subconsciously, my way of expressing gratitude to the gracious audiences who not only tolerated but embraced the free-verse poems I introduced to, or imposed upon, the Elko stages. Off the record—and as contradictory as this may sound—I occasionally enjoy writing the rhymed-'n'-metered lines, and reciting them—my own as well as those of the lariati *and* literati masters—every bit as much as I revel in the open-ended lines. And then there are my song lyrics, *all* of which rhyme. As I inform my most inquisitive listeners, "If it rhymes, it's a song, and if not, it's a poem." *With* exceptions, of course.

Yes, the lyrics—we'll get to them soon, but for now let's stick to the non-rhymers. Prior to participating in the 2005 Elko Cowboy Poetry Gathering, your nineteenth consecutive appearance, you earlier attended a ceremony at the Montana State Capital in Helena where you received the Governor's Arts Award for Literature. I find the juxtaposition of the two, seemingly-paradoxical events fascinating and enchanting—in no small part because previous recipients of the award include a number of Montana's foremost literary dignitaries. You've remarked often that you have one foot fighting for a toe-hold purchase in the literati world and the other hoof planted firmly in the lariati arena. What's your comfort level with that stance?

Thanks for mentioning the brace of humbling honors—nineteen Elkos (twenty-four now, actually), and the Governor's Award—in the same positive tone. And, yes, I'm finally at peace with my position, my calling, after years of feeling disoriented, of being pulled in what I'd sometimes misjudge as opposing directions. What's contributed to my ease, thank goodness, is the abandonment, the devaluing, of inane concepts such as validation, status, fame, and, again, hierarchy. Note that I do not include *fortune*. I'd still like to make some serious mazuma—preferably from my writing, but I'll take it any way I can get it just short of my tongue-in-cheek threat to institute a UniPoet Paladin-For-Hire Hit Man web site. Money means time, and time is the Fort Knox from which I make eight-figure withdrawals, allowing me the solitude and peace in which to revel and wallow "In My Craft Or Sullen Art," to quote the title of a Dylan Thomas poem—a poem I not-so-incidentally recited to the boisterous delight of a sozzled audience in a Swansea pub, one of our U.K. Cowboy Poetry Tour venues, in 1994. I live for the page not for the stage—but let's talk about that later. So if you've heard me tout *ad nauseam* the literati-lariati stance, then you've certainly heard me reconcile any discord between them with my proclamation that, first and foremost, we are all students of the Human Being on Planet Earth School of Poetry. Or, far more precise, "the *Living Being*...." Chances are, the connections between human poetry and the poetry of whales or elephants, parrots or tree frogs, are a lot greater than we'd have ever predicted. In any case, I take seriously what I've deemed my responsibility, my mission, to effect, whenever I'm in front of an audience, harmony between whatever factions might be rearing their ugly hearts. If you tactfully or surreptitiously "afflict the comfortable" after *first* establishing a small parcel of common, philosophical / political / emotional / intellectual / spiritual ground during a presentation or performance of your art, you do the world we live in some good. You "make it a better place," to quote the mantra of a dear friend, Larry Biehl. You give something back to the universe, which, I choose to believe, makes the Muses either bow Their heads in reverence or yodel in orgasmic delight. I've had it with all these sons-a-bitching critics out there flaunting their D-8 Cat heavy-equipment beginner-certificates as they gouge discordant chasms between so-called *folk* and so-called *fine* art. I no longer buy into that insecure need for designation and distinction. If this all sounds anarchistic-to-the-max, good—you've heard, with absolute lucidity, the UniPoet Paladin-For-Hire Hit Man facet of my cowboy-schizoid split personality.

UniPoet?

Shit, I wish I'd not brought it up. When they collared the Unabomber, Ted Kaczynski, outside of Lincoln, Montana—fifty crow-flown miles from where I was holed-up and writing poems at the time in a dilapidated ranch house on Flat Creek in the foothills of the Rocky Mountain Front—I was relieved that they captured the guy, of course, but mortified that he had made camp for all those terrorist years in our beloved state, in *my* domain. Furthermore, not only was he a fellow advocate of manual typewriters, but his last name sports the identical end-rhyme as mine. Sure enough, it wasn't long after, in the midst of making someone's acquaintance, I began to hear, "oh, so you're from Montana and, well, ah-hum, please forgive my asking, but you don't happen to be related to that Unabomber fella do you?" At first, I politely responded, "No, not by a long shot." After a while, my warped sense of humor rode roughshod over my good sense, and I began to quip, "You bet I am—I'm his long-lost far-more-maniacally-Luddite cousin, the Uni*Poet." I confess with much embarrassment that I couldn't resist the temptation to adapt this to a shtick I delivered from the stage. And thus the handle, UniPoet, stuck—mostly in cowpoke poetry circles—and became part of the BIZARzyski persona, for which I am the first to apologize: no disrespect, but rather my deepest sympathy, to Theodore Kaczynski's victims, those dead *and* living. I hope it's understood that my explosive salvos are made of words—poems, not manifestos—intended to heal, not to harm.

Once more, let's circle back. How did the Elko folks find you? Let's talk Elko, talk rodeo, talk rodeo poetry, then and now, The Good, the Bad, and the Ugly, "the truth, the whole truth, and nothing but the truth."

The first I recall hearing about Elko—shorthand for "The National Cowboy Poetry Gathering" held there—was from Bill Kittredge, who delivered the keynote address at the second event in 1986. Bill's writing is fed, or informed, via the deep taproot of his ranch-raised pedigree. He landed back in Missoula bragging about the blast-from-his-past Elko encounter. Soon thereafter, I became a short-time colleague of Bill's at the University of Montana where I taught poetry in the creative writing program. I'm guessing he was the one who arranged a reading for Wally McRae in the Main Hall, in the very room where I last heard Dick Hugo read *and* recite poetry. I'd known about McRae because of his high-profile, anti-coal mining stance in eastern Montana, and had seen him on the news, speaking from the tailgate of his pickup while feeding bulls. With his thick, burled hands, shoein'-

anvil shoulders, chiseled Scotsman face, and smoker's growl of a voice, he looked and sounded *precisely* like the guy you'd pluck from the sidelines to become your steadfast friend in the middle of a brawl at the Bison during the Miles City Bucking Horse Sale. Moreover, I pegged as brilliant both his sensibilities and his thinking. During Wally's reading, I found myself enthralled with the intros to, and stories behind, his poetry, while, at the same time, I found myself annoyed by the humdrum meter and mostly predictable end-rhyme delivery of the work. After the presentation, we gathered at the East Gate Lounge and Liquor Store—of book party "re-supply" fame I mentioned earlier—Missoula's watering hole for *serious* writers, where I more than likely, in trying to make conversation with McRae, committed the definitive sacrilege of the sage and range, the capital offense against ranch culture etiquette, by asking how many head of cattle he ran on his outfit. *If*, in fact, I was guilty of this atrocious faux pas, I'd like to take this opportunity to thank Wallace in print here, over three decades long-overdue, for his absolution—for agreeing to read with tinhorn-gunsel me a few months later on campus in the Student Union lounge. I'd like to express my gratitude also to whomever conceived of presenting us as a dichotomous duet. Professor Bill Bevis distinguished our "literati meets the lariati" watershed event thusly in his introduction—titled "Words and Space"—to the poetry section in *The Last Best Place: A Montana Anthology*, published in 1988 and edited, no less, by Bill Kittredge and Annick Smith:

> One of the best readings I've heard in years was in Missoula, with Paul Zarzyski, modern poet and bronc rider, and Wally McRae, cowboy poet and rancher, sharing the stage. But while both poets were excellent and the shared reading a success, I was also aware of how difficult it is for the ear to move from cowboy poetry to modern poetry. You either expect rhyme and regular rhythm, or you don't; you either expect narrative, or you don't. The reading set me to thinking about Montana and its poetry, and at first I suspected that cowboy poetry probably dominated the scene until the Second World War and that slowly, after Dick Hugo came in 1964, modern poetry took over.

Things are not that simple, however; old issues of *Frontier* show a variety of modern styles during the 1920s and 1930s, and cowboy poets are now gaining national fame. Each kind of poetry—modern and cowboy—has different roots and aims.

Within months of our Missoula gig, Wally conspired with Mike Korn to add me to the troupe repping for Montana at the third annual Elko Gathering. I still maintain that it was all a set-up to determine how the Elko audience would respond to a poetic form so foreign to their ear—that Korn and McRae used me as bait, chum. These are extremely astute men, mind you, and they certainly knew all too well that if cowboy poetry didn't make room for more diverse voices it would soon incur artistic stasis and, shortly thereafter, become insipid daisy fodder. I was thirty-six years old, had just ridden the Montana Pro-Rodeo Circuit Finals, was still in great shape, and likely looked as if I could pool-cue my way out of a saloon full of irritated cowboy-poetry traditionalists, so McRae and Korn did not have to fear for my life. I know they figured themselves in a no-lose situation—if the crowds embraced my work, they'd take the credit for such a wide-vista'd, far-reaching vision, and if not, they'd disavow any responsibility, and probably pin it on Kittredge. The rest is serendipitous history. I wish I could have been there—even as a spectator—for the first two go-rounds in 1985 and 1986. Fact is, a fine, fine poet *and* genuine cowpuncher from New Mexico, Drum Hadley, debuted free verse at the kick-off Gathering. Rumor has it my candidacy was actually discussed, but nixed on the grounds that I was merely a rodeo cowboy and worse, a rodeo cowboy out of the academy.

So how was your maiden Elko trip?

"Trip," indeed. It's somewhat akin to that sixties dictum, "If you remember it, you weren't there." I do recall reading, not reciting, and likely re-reading a six-pack of poems, including "The Heavyweight Champion Pie-Eating Cowboy of the West" and "Escorting Grammy to the Potluck Rocky Mountain Oyster Feed at Bowman's Corner," all from *The Make-Up of Ice*. I'd never before presented my work to a filled, thousand-seat auditorium, which upped the decibels of the applause by ten-fold. Each performance was as rewarding as riding the bronc Whiskey Talks to the pay window two weeks earlier at the Montana Pro-Rodeo Circuit Finals in Great Falls. And speaking of Whiskey Talks, after the Gathering I wrote a poem titled "Martini McRae and Whiskey Zarzyski: A Brace of Blackjack Aces"—about getting soused and losing big at the Stockman's Casino. I'll bet a double-sawbuck that Wally and I came damn close to trumping Kittredge's record-breaking bar bill of the previous year. Moreover, I crossed trails with a hundred or so kindred spirits, many of whom I'm still in touch with today.

I think you'll agree that, hard as we so often try, we seldom can revisit, or recreate, moments that magical. What's beckoned you back— for twenty-five consecutive Gatherings.

Did you bring your bedroll? Maybe a few anecdotes can best address your question. I'll begin with the most unusual of my tenure. Ten Gatherings or so ago, during a Friday evening show in the main auditorium, I recited "The Whale in My Wallet." Its subject matter is light-years removed from what most would deem "cowboy." As part of my intro, I employ a pair of tidbits I may have clipped from L. M. Boyd newspaper columns: First, "Scientific tests suggest whales and cows evolved from a common land ancestor," followed by, "Whales' songs rhyme." I also offer up how a friend, Mary Kathleen (Kitty) Collins, who I first met at the Gathering in 1987, sends a special Christmas gift each year, an adoption certificate for the humpback whale named Stub; how humpbacks have unique fingerprint-like markings on the underside of their flukes by which researchers identify them on the open seas; thus, how I might, for example, receive an occasional newsletter stating that "Stub was seen surface-feeding in twenty-foot swells," and, therefore, I can rest assured that my adopted son is flourishing, prospering out there among his fellow leviathans. "Obviously," I tell the audience, "you can't keep a picture of an entire fifty-foot, forty-ton whale in your wallet," and so...

We're talking humpbacks, not greenbacks,
but I'm still sitting fat

packing only his flukes—biggest fingerprints
you ever saw high-fiving me
or, should I say, *two-highing* me out of the gray
Atlantic—Sable Island to Stellwagon Bank
to New York Bight—or maybe out of the blue
Caribbean, off Puerto Rico, off Haiti,
off the Grenadines. He moves around a bit,
this ubiquitous humpback, this quasi-
Quasi Moto, I suppose, of his pod,
after some three-story-tall titanic
propeller or snaggle-toothed denizen
out of Davy Jones's Locker
chewed his dorsal fin off his back, and left him
with his anatomical namesake—you guessed it—
Stub. Not Neptune, Rigadoon, Tom Cruise, Sing-a-tune,
not even peg-legged Blackbeard or Captain Hook,
but just plain old monosyllabic-ugly, *Stub*,
like the nickname of a Polish-Italian hit man,
Stub Podgurski, *Stub* Lagunowski, *Stub* Mitolio—
monikers from my hometown phone book!...

Anyway, you get the picture and, depending on your funny bone's sensibilities, you maybe can imagine how the piece brings down the house. The following encounter concerning this poem occurred during one of the years I'd flown into Elko early to conduct either a writing or a cooking workshop. I had likely put in a rigorous seven- or eight-day shift and was exhausted to the marrow—"crowd-foundered," to use a term I stake claim to having coined. It was the final day of the Gathering, I'd probably slept less than a couple blotto'd hours, and I was in desperate need of a quiet breakfast—everything, Rice Crispies included, set on *mute*. I directed the waitress to seat me at a high-backed corner booth where I faced away from the room and buried my Polish-Eye-talian pan damn near eyebrows-deep beneath the wide brim of my appropriately named Resistol (pronounced "resist all") hat. I was determined to eat, for a change, my ham-'n'-eggs warm. But just at the instant that I began to feel some success in achieving this feat, I noticed through the corner of my eye a figure sliding in next to me. I no doubt turned with a glower, but before I could swallow my mouthful of hash browns, a quite lovely woman apologetically said, "I know, I *know*—I'm from California—I know how you must need your space, but I just couldn't leave town without telling you that this is my first Gathering—I do some reining-horse riding and write a few poems—and although I didn't know what to expect here in Elko, *the last* thing I could have *ever* imagined experiencing was to sit in that auditorium last night and hear a cowboy poet recite a poem about *my* adopted humpback whale!" It was Stub's mom! I mean, if I'm Stub's surrogate father, here was his mother. Carla Meyer told me she worked as "a dialect coach" in the movie business. Film buff that I am, I replied, "Would I recognize any of the pictures you've been involved in?" She was in fact flying from Elko back to Chicago to wrap up duties on *Road to Perdition* with Tom Hanks and Paul Newman. Months later, I sat alone in the theater after everyone had exited during the slow rolling of the credits and, sure enough, Carla was listed. We've stayed in touch somewhat over the years. I've pleaded with her to please inform the likes of Jodi Foster, Halle Barry, Ellen Barkin, Salma Hayek, and Hillary Swank of my deep, Rodeo-Poet affection for these extremely talented, ravishing women, but so far have not heard word one from a single actress. All silliness aside, only in Elko have I experienced such enchanting encounters with such a widely-diverse cross section of enthusiasts for all things western and smithed into words.

So these kinds of surprise encounters occur every year?

Pretty much. In the early 1990s, I wound up sharing the stage with renowned Russian bard, Yevtushenko. After that Gathering, I wrote "Yevgeny Alexandrovich Yevtushenko—Cowboy Poet," in which I celebrate, and ironically lament or indict, his presence:

> ...you capriole from podium,
> glide, prance, pivot, swoop, whirl, as if the room
> effervesces with pinkish iridescent bubble-
> bath bubbles shaped like Cupid hearts
> popping to the hot soft guttural
> touch of your phonics, of your skinny fingers
> sculpting and scripting into sexy metaphor
> the palpable air of our women's longing. You tempt them
> away from our horse lather and leather pheromones

into the surrealistic—lure
them with your somniloquous lips. How dare you kiss
their thinnest skin, their rice-paper cheeks,
the silken backs of their hands gone limp
to your lines' feminine feline endings
gently penetrating their capillary
yearnings? How dare you
mesmerize us men into applauding
your pilferage?

We cowboy poets were left, in Cossack poet Yevtushenko's wake, ashamed of our domestication, our civility, our tameness. It might've been during the closing night of that very same Gathering when a wounded Wally McRae—maybe after single-handedly attempting to uphold our rogue, Casanova-cowpuncher-poet reputations—phoned my room at 5:00 a.m. as I was frantically packing to catch our oh-dark-thirty Sunday flight out of Elko, to Mayday me thusly: "Paul. This is Wally. I'm in a world of shit. I can't find my hat, my wallet, or my airline ticket."

More?

The Western Folklife Center, manned and especially *womaned* by a staff of the brightest, most ambitious and innovative people ever to come together to orchestrate an artistic event—we're talking Cowpoke Woodstock, mind you—has partnered us up in Elko with performers from various horse cultures across the globe. The Australian drovers, the Hawaiian paniolos, the Mexican vaqueros, to name a most obvious few. Several years ago we were joined by the Mongolian horsemen, with whom I and Henry Real Bird—in my opinion, currently the most significant voice of our cowboy poet "tribe"—were cast for the closing Saturday night performance. I've jokingly referred to it as "your Polish-Mafioso-Rodeo-Poet, Mongolian Horseman, Crow Indian show." The Mongolian troupe spoke little English, so I asked their interpreter to prompt them, at my signal, to spread out behind me across stage. I think we coaxed Henry up there as well. My idea was that I'd recite my boom-along poem, "Why I Like BUTTE!" The interpreter relayed my instructions to shout in unison "BUTTE!" whenever I turned to them and drew my imaginary six-guns. Picture the seven or eight of them in full colorful regalia, all smiles and ebullience. I'd turn and they, much faster on the draw than I, would pull their thumb-hammered forefinger Colt .45s and yell BUTTE! each of the dozen or so times the refrain sounded off in the poem. I laughed so hard I forgot the lines. The audience was on their knees and clutching their diaphragms. For the rest of the night—2:00, 3:00, 4:00 a.m.—whenever I'd see one of the mostly vertically-challenged Mongolians, they'd be on their tiptoes in attempts to rise above the rollicking, drunk, Stockman Casino horde and boom with laughter in my direction, BUTTE! BUTTE! BUTTE! Soon thereafter—and far-fetched as this might sound to someone not having been there—I began suggesting that maybe that single-syllable nonsensical word, which connected people from cultures thousands of miles apart in, of all the unlikely microcosmic Meccas, Elko, Nevada—that *just maybe* that word, BUTTE!, acted miraculously and momentarily as the definitive synonym for HOPE! or PEACE! or LOVE!

BUTTE!

Or ELKO! You know, the annual event has graced thousands of lives with a sense of, and need for, pilgrimage. Most of the attendees, both performers and audience alike, are more than willing to leave their egos back at the ranch or office or wherever—to show up, hats in hands, with heads bowed in reverence and humility. Few—very few—regard themselves too highly as star performers or star patrons. I mean, in light of how brief our time is here in this dimension, as well as how readily the majority of us are replaced after we check out—our talents or vocations or functions or whatever fulfilled by the next in line—why gloat over our own notoriety or celebrity status? One year a famous fiddlin' figurehead took the main stage and deemed it his cultural, rural, jingoistic, homophobic propriety to tell certain jokes. The audience revolted—complaints were both rabid and rampant, I'm proud to say. That entertainer never returned. Others who've misjudged our eclectic bunch were also set straight and/or sent packing.

You make it sound a bit overly idyllic.

You're right—thanks for keeping me honest. I'm forced to admit a recent developing polarity, a palpable divisiveness, especially in the wake of both George Bush's "Cowboy Politics" presidency and the election of Barack Obama. And I've had it with the anti-Obama Klan (yes, *Klan)* erroneously pegging me—because of my cowboy appearance, I'm postulating—as a born-again racist. There's a big difference between my black hat and a white hood, goddamnit. Thank your lucky stars, I'll spare you the jokes with which I've been assaulted. Wally and I have talked often about how our garb has become one more *uniform* associated with that worn by the conservative right. It dampens my soul to acknowledge the degree of bigotry still thriving in the cowboy West.

We know that you supported Natalie Maines of the Dixie Chicks, who denounced, from a Great Britain stage, President George W. Bush, and thereby incurred a firestorm of animosity from fans and fellow musicians alike. We know also that you sided with Oprah, who prevailed in a lawsuit filed against her by the Texas Cattlemen's Association after she said on her show that she, in light of unsanitary slaughterhouse conditions, would never eat another hamburger. In metaphorical sync with the latter, it seems you're not afraid to liberally (no pun intended) "bite the hand that feeds you," considering that you make the bulk of your living as a cowboy poet. Is it true that your politics cost the Western Folklife Center a membership donation from a woman who took umbrage with, as she perceived it, the lack of patriotism in your anti-war stance?

That's the rumor. But I'm not shouldering the guilt, or gratification, solo on this one. I can name hundreds—poets, musicians, audience, *and* staff, alike—who feel as I do about all of our most recent wars. I agree with the Patron Saint of Cowboy Artists, Charles M. Russell, who notched his anti-war, poetic six-shooter with the following verse: "If merriment be ignorance / And War is wisdom's school / With gory blades as teachers / I am, thank the saints, a fool." My dad served during WW II, and was as proud of his service as anything he'd accomplished, including guiding his three sons toward honorable lives. Several years ago, in tribute to Veteran's Day, the *Ironwood Daily Globe* saluted those local vets who were interested in submitting a photo and brief comment. Dad asked if I'd help him with the latter, so we talked for a long while about his sentiments. I spent a much longer while centrifuging them into the following, which he confirmed was exactly how he felt: "Serving during wartime involves three objectives: 1) complete the mission; 2) return home alive and as physically and emotionally intact as possible; and 3) move the world toward war*lessness*." We achieved the first goal in WWII because so many men and women sacrificed the second objective. As for the third, the jury, unfortunately, seems not only to be out but forever AWOL. I was raised lovingly by a patriot who believed, as many true patriots do, that peace is the highest form of patriotism. Look at this picture of Dad in 1947—he was one handsome sailor…(pause)…sorry….

You want to take a breather?

No, thanks—let's finish this round, hopefully with a flurry. It's been my observation that the majority of people involved in the arts are among the most *non*-conservative, *non*-fundamentalist, *non*-bigoted, *non*-greed-mongering, *non*-hawkish, and *non*-theocratic folks inhabiting this great country. In sync with this observation, I believe the revival of cowboy poetry and music has flourished for a quarter century and continues, more or less, to prosper, *because* of the visions of a group of non-conservative, non-hawkish, non-theocratic, incredibly bright, egalitarian folklorists and / or educated enthusiasts: Jim Griffith, Charlie Seemann, Meg Glaser, Carol Edison, Debbie Fant, Mike Korn, Hal Cannon, Elizabeth Dear, Andrea Graham, Christina Barr, Darcy Minter, to name just a few in no particular order. To couch it in the simplest, most humble terms, we poets and singers are not, by any stretch of the imagination, the brightest stars in this galaxy, although we're more often than not the ones credited with the utmost radiance. In contrast I can affirm that 99 percent of the folklorists and their staffs, and the presenters and volunteers and board members and advocates, would run for cover before allowing anyone to distinguish them. To put it most bluntly, were it not for the Western Folklife Center, opportunities to stand on a public stage for cowboy poets would likely be altogether nonexistent. I'd have probably taught one or two years of junior college comp classes before being sentenced to a stint in "the lodge"—*Rancho Deluxe* redux—for whatever desperate non-violent crime I'd committed in order to focus full-time on my work rather than a job. We cowboy entertainers owe a tremendous debt of appreciation to the National Endowment for the Arts and to numerous other *liberal* arts organizations—to their visionaries, their advocates, their staffs. I'm basking as we speak in the brilliant afterglow of two recent events I witnessed on television: the first, Bruce Springsteen—sitting in the Kennedy Center balcony with President and First Lady Obama—while musician friends performed his hits in tribute to the 2009 Kennedy Award Bruce received; and secondly, K. D. Lang, at the opening ceremony of the Vancouver Winter Olympics, singing Leonard Cohen's prayerful song "Hallelujah." Both moments, thanks to the potency of the creative soul, graced me with infusions of hope for humankind's possibilities, our potential for goodness.

You obviously love, as well as feel an eternal indebtedness toward, the Elko presenters and the audiences they've attracted and fostered. Can I nudge you toward a recitation of your poems in celebration of cowboy poetry and cowboy poetry audiences?

I can't even begin to imagine the wealth of friendship and wisdom, artistic satisfaction and joy, I'd be without, should the past twenty-five years of my participation in this celebration of western culture and tradition be suddenly erased. I've crossed trails with thousands—yes, thousands!—of loving, passionate people because of the cowboy stages. People who worship the power and beauty of words every bit as much as I do. Good, sweet beings—givers, not takers, for the most part. People who'll laugh with you one minute and weep with you the next. Emotionally honest people. What a gift bestowed upon me from the Old Cowpoke Cosmos—what a glorious eternal gift. You bet, I'd be honored to recite the brace of poems you're requesting—no "nudge" needed. First, a piece written in response to the romantic Larry Pirnie painting adorning the year 2000 Elko Cowboy Poetry Gathering poster. A poem, furthermore, that Wylie Gustafson adapted verbatim to an elegant melody he created. And then, an homage to our audience:

Grace

In the soft low light up high
Where love has always thrived and will

Forever yearn for the colorful hover—a brush stroke
Of words out of the West—we still "want
Free life," we still "want fresh air."

And as millenniums meander by
Like birthdays to the earth, what thrill
A saffron blade of grass, blue sage, scrub oak
Still brings us on our daily jaunt
Across the land, our daily poem, our prayer.

Gratitude

In the height of this poetry moment
Right people, right place, and right time,
The universe stirs with chevrons of words
While The Zenith Cathedral bells chime.

In the heat of this poetry moment,
Hoist your grails to Beauty and Truth—
Through fire and smoke, wild not broke,
One more round from The Geyser of Youth.

In the heart of this poetry moment,
To your tempo, your rhythm, your flow—
With ink from my veins, *Three Cheers!* in quatrains
For the spirit *you've* brought to this show.

*Please, just one more close encounter of the Elko kind? I'm
itching to know if I actually heard you say, "cooking workshop?"*

Does canederli (pronounced, "can-'ay-der-lee") ring any cow-
boy cuisine dinner bells for you? Italian dumplings? My noni,
Angelina Paternoster, emigrated, pregnant with my mother,
Delia, from a mountain village in northern Italy—Tregiovo, the
Trentino-Alto Adige region. Found her name on the wall at Ellis
Island. I'm guessing the dumpling recipe, which Mom prepared
often, originated in Austria, just over the border. I've conducted
a trio of Rodeo Poet, *Cast* Iron Chef, workshops in Elko. One
of them included, if memory serves me—which it should not,
considering the gallons of screw-top Chianti we guzzled—venison

heart gravy over *polenta slaccha*, or soft polenta. The woman I put in charge of stirring, of strong-arming, the industrial-sized, stainless steel fumarole of seething, wheezing, spitting cornmeal broke a wooden spoon, stout as an ax handle, in half. That was quite the epicurean experience, alright, but nowhere near the free-for-all that evolved on the Day of the Runaway / Renegade Canederli. My mother's recipe calls for dried bread shards mixed with eggs, flour, milk, Genoa salami cubes, garlic, of course, and Italian parsley. You mix the concoction in a large bowl with your bare hands, and then form tennis-ball-sized spheres, which you spoon into a broth of boiled beef, celery, carrots, and onions, sans said contents. Usually twenty minutes in the broth suffices, depending on circumference. After my students emptied several Gallo gallons, their canederli ranged everywhere in size on the orbicular spectrum from golf ball to bocci ball, which, as you can imagine, made the critical boiling times a mite tricky. At the most frenetic point, I believe I caught an apparitional glimpse of Rod "Eyebrows" Serling stepping through the steam and delivering his signature, "Imagine, if you will," line. Canederli are served in a bowl with the broth and, if desired, a generous grating of Asiago cheese. My mom would cool and cube the beef—generally a cheap roast cut—and serve it as a side salad with raw sweet onion, oil, and wine vinegar (dark red kidney beans optional). In Elko, as long as beef was involved, we figured we could call it "cowboy." After three hours of hard drinking, raucous laughter, haphazard attention to recipe details (twenty-five or more of us bumper-to-bumper in a hot kitchen—me and my sous-chef, songwriter *paesano* Tom Perlman the only males *I* remember), we ate our delectable chuck, then staggered, fat-'n'-sassy, back to our motel rooms. I stopped by the Western Folklife Center watering hole for a nightcap and will never forget seeing face-up on the bar the handout I'd Xeroxed for the class—Mom's recipe, side-by-side with a picture of her beaming her effervescent Tirolean smile, a single canederli cradled in one uplifted palm, a drink gripped in her other hand, and, in the foreground on the kitchen table, her big breadboard bedecked with a batch of Italian dumplings marching, so to speak, in formation. I'd taken the photo a month earlier in her kitchen at 505 Poplar, when visiting for Christmas and a snap course in the art of the canederli. Mom still laughs and laughs when I tell her about her picture on the bar in Elko— *only* in Elko.

Round 3

Your approach to the page, the process, the germination or conception of the poem—where do they come from?

Hank Williams said, "I pick up a pen and God moves it." Keith Richards proclaimed, "Nobody creates anything. It's there and you just fucking grab hold of it." For me, neither of those two simplistic responses even begin to address such a complicated question. I say they don't all come from the heavens, nor are they all just there. "Where do they come from?" Out of the luminous mind, out of the heart of darkness, out of the gloaming, out of the gloom; out of the wide-open, out of the shadows, out of the deep, and the shallows; out of the magma, out of the blood—both artery and vein—out of the xylem and phloem, out of the mighty river, the meandering brook, the trickling spring, out of the purl of anything and everything liquid, out of the mass of all that is solid, out of the vapors of gas; out of fusion, fission, alchemy, the real and surreal, ether and essence, reasoning and miracle; out of the eye of the hurricane, "somewhere over the rainbow," the land of Oz, left field; out of the organic and synthetic —steel, iron, plastic, glass, bone, skin, branch, bark, cell, atom, molecule, proton, neutron, gut, stardust, brain, marrow of the soul— out of the timelessness of all time, out of the noise of all silence, out of the finite of all infinity, and on and on and eternally on…but, at its very best, always out of and into *The Glorious Commotion Of It All,* to echo the title of one of my spoken-word CDs.

As well as to echo "Face-To-Face," your opening poem in Wolf Tracks on the Welcome Mat? *Care to read it?*

Sure.

> Out of nowhere, you find yourself
> placed daily before the fortress,
> rustic logs throbbing
> something from within
> you vaguely recognize
> as music—so primal,
> so otherworldly in its purpose,
> you are at once drawn closer,
> cautioned back. Succumb
> to ugly logic, to mean-spirited
> reason, or religion,
> and you, believing you shun
> merely the unknown, will flee
> unwittingly from beauty. Trust the blood,
> however, waltzing to four-part harmony
> within the heart, and you will be moved
> to witness, through the chinking's
> thin fissures, the shadows
> of the enchanted. Then, and only then,
> might you choose to follow
> a force you'll lovingly call your soul
> through huge swinging doors
> thrown open to the glorious
> commotion of it all.

So then how do you greet or receive them?

That one's tougher to field. If you posed this question to a thousand poets, I suspect you'd get at least 998 diverse responses. For *me,* first off, it's mostly a matter of showing up in poetic gear, of being there in poetic mode. My eight antennas, after thirty-eight years of writing, are always extended, but in varying degrees of telescopic length. Most poets would agree that it has little to do with seeking out material or experience or worthy moments—that it's the farthest thing from scientific research, from Arctic explorations, African safaris, archaeological digs. At the opposite, extreme end of the spectrum, I've never found it very fruitful to institute a disciplined writing schedule, to show up day-in, day-out, and confront the blank page, stare it down like Davy Crockett did the "b'ar," (heaven bless Fess Parker) until it gives in, grins back at you, licks your face. Although I do concede that either of the above approaches could work wonderfully for writers far more methodical than I. My way, *simply*, is to make a leap of faith with those eight antennas as outstretched and tuned-in as possible to the daily chaos—not all of it unfortunate chaos. For me it's all warp and weft—an intricate bird's nest or Navajo weaving, at its best; a casting reel's tangled backlash, a cosmic cluster-*bumfuggle* at its worst. I'm talking about a million moments in any given day—how they connect or disconnect and which ones, if any, call out the loudest (dog-whistle quiet sometimes), rise above the thick cloud of dust over a milling herd, reach out, grab hold of my ear or eye or windpipe, titillate my nape hairs, make my synapses snap and crackle like—to borrow a line from my poem, "Flamenca Duende,"—"hot wires flailing wild in a gale." The thing is, your **Poetry Welcomed** or **Welcome Poetry** mat better always be out and prominent. Better yet, a fuchsia-'n'-chartreuse cursive neon sign flashing, "Mi Casa Es Su Casa" to Poetry in every window. Add to the above lurings a marquee above each door sporting in big black mantra block letters those four *F*s I mentioned earlier: FEARLESSNESS! FREEDOM! FIERCENESS! FUN! If you're residing within the city limits, you should discover daily, dangling from your front door knob, a housing code violation warning. Make any sense?

I think so. However, I expected a more, shall we say, formulaic or tangible or concrete answer. More scholarly, maybe? More literary?

Turn the Bakelite dials of your tympanums—connected to the transistors or vacuum tubes of your middle and inner ear—all to their prospective word music channels, Superglue the boogers there for good, and let the rhythms and lilts and riffs of the syllables dictate your daily cadences as you move poetically through life.

So many musical words and so little time to juxtapose them infinitely.

Okay. That covers the music, but what about the message? Didn't Hugo say, "In every poem there's a constant battle going on between the music and the message, and in the very best poems, neither ever wins"?

Yes he did—almost verbatim, I believe. But he also suggested that during the crafting of a poem the music blazes trail for the message, so to speak. He was echoing the sentiments of hundreds of poets who wrote before him, including Ezra Pound, who said, "Poetry atrophies when it gets too far from music." Therefore, by placing the heaviest concentration on the music, the poet stands the best chance of allowing the poem to say what *it* has to say, in opposition to the poet's encroachment or intrusion. Dick put it clearly for me when he declared, "Poems are like people—if you give them a chance, they'll tell you what they have to say... if you listen to people long enough, they'll tell you what's on their minds." I'm not much of a horseman but I believe there's a bit of a connection, however remote, between the poet's and the equine maestro's applied psychology and philosophy and, perhaps, spirituality. Years back I wrote a poem which attempts to speak to this correlation. I dedicated it to one of the West's wisest *amansadores* (horse trainers) and arguably the finest reciter of classic cowboy poetry, Randy Rieman. It's not an easy poem, whatever that means. It's titled, "The Horseman, the Poet, the Code, the Horse."

I'd like to hear it and, while you're at it, it seems to me that a lot of what you've been emphasizing reflects or ricochets off another ars poetica *piece from* Wolf Tracks..."*Putting The Rodeo Try Into Cowboy Poetry.*" *But first let's hear "The Horseman..."?*

The Horseman, the Poet, the Code, the Horse

> Sizing up each other's hearts, and caught
> off guard by ripples of their own
> reflections, the poet reveres the horseman
> as high priest, the horseman beholds

the poet as wizard. In the round pen
with a gentle colt, this trinity of hearts
beats most lovingly because, with love,
nobody becomes the broken. They delight in the flying
lead change of fresh blood, fresh words,
circulating within horse, within horseman and poet,
within this circular cowboy universe
where no two boot heels or hooves—like stars,
like snowflakes or meteorites
or the blacksmith's hammer striking hot iron—
have ever fallen with the same grace,
gravity, fervor, and force
exactly to the same circle. The two men agree that,
for strangers, they agree much
too eagerly. And then, wide-eyed, again
in harmony, they nod to the synchronized wisdom
of their mentors—Hugo, Dorrance—showing them how
"it's you feeling of the horse, the poem,
and the poem, the horse, feeling of you."
The horseman hands the poet an old bridle—worn
Jeremiah Watt bit and braided reins
he cowboyed with in five states. The poet
hands the horseman a thin book of works
he wrote between rodeos he rode in one-dream
three-bar towns. Seldom has either man known
an *adios* so slow. In unison they turn
toward the round corral, sudden wind
imitating the sound of wings. Angels—some say
ranahan angels, disguised as fresh western air,
will perch the circle of top rails. Hands still
clasped in their long good-bye,
horseman and poet come full-circle
to this message, to A Blessing, to friendship
lit at the withers between earth and sky.

"Between earth and sky?" As in, Between Earth And Sky: Poets
of the Cowboy West—*the magnificent anthology edited by your
friend Anne Heath Widmark, and published by W.W. Norton
in 1995? Good steal. Now how about that other* ars *cowpoke
poetica piece, "...Rodeo Try..."?*

Putting the Rodeo Try into Cowboy Poetry

Let's begin with the wildest landscape, space
inhabited by far more of them
than our own kind and, yes, we *are* talking
other hearts, other stars. Fall in love with all
that is new born—universe, seedling, dawn,
human, foal, calf. Love equally
the seasons, know each sky has meaning,
winter-out the big lonesomes, the endless
horizons our hopes sink beyond
once every minute, sometimes
seeming never to rise
again for air or light,
for life. Fall *madly* in love
with earth's fickle ways. Heed
hard the cosmos cues, the most
minuscule pulsings, subtle nods—no heavy-
handed tap or poke, nothing muscular,
no near-death truths revealed, no telephone
or siren screaming us out of sleep
at 3 a.m. Forget revelation.
Forgive religion. Let's believe instead in song
birds or Pegasus, the only angels
we'll ever need. Erase for good
inspiration from our Random Bunk-
House Dictionaries, from our petty heads
and pretty ambitions. Poetry is not
the grace or blessing we pray for—Poetry
is the Goddess for whom
we croon. Sing and surely we shall see
how she loves our music in any key—
any color, any creed, any race, any breed. Rhyme
if the muse or mood moves us
to do so. Go slow. Walk
then trot, lope then rock
and roll for even a split second, our souls
in the thundergust middle, the whole

world suddenly *getting western,*
pitching a tizzy fit, our horses
come uncorked—just as we were
seriously beginning to think
we savvied the salty? To believe we could
ever turn this stampede,
like steers, into a milling
circle? Into a civil gathering of words?

Being a fan of James Wright I caught, as well, the title reference to his exquisite horse poem, "A Blessing," in the closing lines to "The Horseman, the Poet." You've never presented these two works back-to-back?

Not until just now. And I agree—that is indeed a fine James Wright poem.

Who else do you read—who did you read early on?

I actually discovered poetry thanks to David Steingass at the University of Wisconsin–Stevens Point, where I received an undergraduate degree with double majors in Biology and English. David was my first semester composition teacher in the fall of 1969. He introduced me to Paul Zimmer, Dave Etter, Gary Gildner, Diane Wakoski, John Woods, John Knoepfle, Gary Snyder, Wendell Berry, John Haines, and others. I recall especially embracing Haines's early books, *Winter News* and *The Stone Harp,* set mostly in the Alaska backcountry. Also, it just now occurs to me that a few of those wellspring influences— Gildner, Etter, and Zimmer in particular—groomed me with their humorous work for participation on the cowboy stages, such a large facet of that genre focused on the whimsical, the comedic, the stand-up poet, so to speak. And I do not mean this at all in a derisive vein. Steingass left the following year on sabbatical and I shouldered into the sciences. It must have been spring semester of 1972 when, to my advisor's chagrin, I deviated from my chosen curriculum to enroll in a beginning poetry writing class David was offering. My advisor exclaimed, "You don't *need* any more humanities." To which I replied, "On the contrary, I've never needed them *more.*" The "Class II-S" student deferment was keeping me out of 'Nam. I'd won the famous draft lottery with the number twenty-six—where was 51, or better yet, 251 or 351, when it could have literally saved my life? I was weary of the rote of taxonomic terms, the regurgitation of chemical formulas. I needed to seek out the significance of Paul Zarzyski's existence, if any, aboard this planet in the twentieth century. Though I likely would not have characterized it as such back then, I simply wanted to tell *my* stories, to turn up the volume on *my own* one-of-a-kind heartbeat, *my own* unique imagination and / or thinking. The light at the self-discovery intersection had changed overnight from red to a brilliant green. I stomped on the defiance accelerator and never once glanced in the rearview mirror at the flashing lights of authority that I left disappearing in the gravel-spray and smoking rooster tails of burnt rubber. I wrote my first *serious* poetry, albeit thinly crafted, and decided to pick up the minimum credits for an English major while finishing my biology requirements. And then in the winter of 1972 and 1973, I applied to the writing program at the University of Montana. I recall sauntering into Steingass's office and announcing—in the wake of Nixon ending the war, the draft—that I was by-god moving to Montana and that I'd sure like to continue to learn to write poetry but I doubted the two endeavors were in sync with one another. He replied, "You're in luck. The U of M offers a Master of Fine Arts degree in creative writing—one of the top programs in the country." He then went on to lament, however, that my chances of being admitted, with my having written a grand total of maybe a dozen poems, were slim, at best. Poet Gary Thompson was the student representative on the selection committee. He was also a fan of Paul Zimmer's work, and though I do not recall later talking to him in detail about his role, my Zimmer imitations—"Zarzyski Takes the Advice of Horace Greeley," for example—must've piqued his interest. I'm presuming he was my staunchest and maybe lone advocate. I will always remember that moment of jubilation as I read the acceptance letter. That envelope is buried somewhere deep, *deep* in the archives. I was also granted a teaching assistantship. And with Gary's and Quinton Duval's and Hugo's and Madeline DeFrees's encouragement, I discovered and read James Wright, Dylan Thomas, Ray Carver, Jim Harrison, Maxine Kumin, James Dickey, Mary Oliver, Sharon Olds, Philip Levine, Stanley Kunitz, and a hundred other accomplished poets who all informed my work. And then *this* full-circle postscript: Paul Zimmer, the poetry editor at the *University of Georgia Press*, accepted my first book, *The Make-Up of Ice,* for publication a decade later. How's that for connectivity and continuity—Steingass, Zimmer, Duval, Thompson, all with whom I've remained grand friends since the early 1970s.

Let's backtrack. Would you be willing to relate one of those "close encounters of the umpteenth poetic kind" you alluded to early-on in this round? You're moseying or gamboling or traipsing or galloping or blurring at warp ten speed through a run-of-the-mill day, all your dials Superglued into musical place, your eight antennas extended to varying degrees of telescopic penetration out into the musical universe, at least one of them, hopefully, tickling the Muse most anatomically intimately, when suddenly you hear the poem stomping the snow off its galoshes right outside your door on the **Poetry Welcomed** *mat. Then what?*

I could not have pitched the question with more metaphorical, eloquent, enticing acumen, myself. It's no secret that I'm a thrift store junkie—especially on the hunt for cowboy-'n'-Indian kitsch from the 1940s and 1950s. And the primary focus of my collections, as you can see, is the hand-painted cowpoke cravat—flashy western neckties of yore. If you'll excuse a boast, I am the king of the buckin' hoss twister necktie collectors. But I'm drawn, as well, to most any pictorial or, in some cases, abstract, air-brushed classic—the more outrageous / gaudy / weird, the better. A dozen or so years ago, I'm in the St. Vincent de Paul's in Great Falls. It's late. I notice a shopping cart half-filled with shoes, which I identify as that operated by John Jasmann (pronounced Jazz man), a Down syndrome-afflicted employee of St. Vinny's for, at that time, twenty-five years, most of those years spent orchestrating the used shoe department. Johnny, a country-'n'-western music fan, wore headphones as he worked and would oftentimes *sing* (caterwaul) along with whatever song he was listening to. He is also a fellow aficionado of neckties—his signature, a daily, different design dangling from his shoe-filled shopping cart. And on *this* night, my eye catches a wide rayon print sporting a keyboard image from its tip to Johnny's half-hitched rendition of a Windsor knot snubbed to the cart's push bar. I buy the tie, take it home, and, instead of hanging it from one of the two dozen racks on the walls you see here in my writing niche, I lay it alongside my beloved Smith-Corona where it did everything but get up and dance the zoot-suited Lindy before I finally received its cue to write the piece I believe I was destined to write. Fact is, I think I was doing a few rounds on the heavy bag when *it hit me*, and we ain't talking nebulous revelation here—I mean, how much more obvious could it have been that the poem would somehow address music? But the real truth-'n'-beauty nucleus of *the story* evolved via the journey through numerous drafts over a period of months. I walked into St. Vinny's one day in the midst of those rewritings and, as usual, enjoyed my short exchange with John who, I was surprised to note, was sorting shirts and not shoes. Found out that he'd incurred not so much a demotion but more of a lateral move in his employment status after he began to display the shoes and boots in haphazard fashion rather than in matched pairs. I'll bet I struggled through no less than 51 reconstructions of the closing stanza to "Montana Second Hand" before settling for the phrasings, the syntaxes—the rendering—I'm about to recite for you. French poet Paul Valéry said, "A poem is never finished, only abandoned." Never before had I experienced the truth of his words to this extent. It may have had a little to do with an underlying resistance I felt long before I scratched the first note onto the page—probably right from the very moment I unhitched that keyboard tie from John's cart. Who *in hell* did I think I was intruding into a life of which I could not even begin to comprehend the heights of holiness? After reciting the poem for years to cowboy poetry audiences, I met John's brother, Mark, a horseman and cowman head-to-foot, hat-to-boots. Johnny, it turns out, was born on a cattle ranch in the Madison River Valley near Ennis, Montana. Don't ask me how, but I knew all along I was writing a cowboy poem.

Montana Second Hand

Down's syndrome can't hinder the Saint
Vincent de Paul thrift store
troubadour of the shoe department,
John Jasmann, singing his pedal steel guitar
love songs into his rhapsodical
job—sorting used footwear
into rows from his shopping cart piled
high with each day's fresh stock. His photo

album propped open
in the child carrier, Polaroids
showcasing him at work—and his touch
of personal panache, one flashy cravat hanging,
half-hitched, from the cart's push-bar—
he belts out a line of Louisiana Hayride
classic, "...son of a gun
we'll have big fun on the bayou."

                              Hank Williams

lilting hit after hit, John
presses his palms to the Walkman headphones,
as if holding a lover in a long kiss,
and takes wing on the Nashville airwaves
bringing us a little "...how's about cookin'
somethin' up with me."

                         Strange as this may sound,
John stumbled once onto the key of C,
his usual out-of-tune
cacophony turning
suddenly to a melodic
lovely a cappella: "I'm so lo-o-nsome
Iiii could cryyy."

                         Listen—as each shopper,
gawking with awe toward *Shoes,*
pictures some rockabilly god,
some rhythm-'n'-blues aficionado,
maybe Saint Vinny himself,
rolling a ruby-ringed finger
over the solid gold dial
tuned to *Angelic Debut.*

                         May grace taking shape
tangibly in a single line of singing
draw us all one lonesome day
toward the mysterious
display of white shoes
staggered with black boots
across wrought iron racks. There, may each shelf
holding the notes, sharps, flats,
show us how the maestro—excited
by the infinite, cued to the unique
movements we make

arranged together in perfect time—writes
out of all our used lives
one sweet music.

"Maestro"—with an upper-case M implied?

Mick Vernon, of the Green Bay Packer fan brotherhood, as well as of the Monterey Cowboy Poetry and Music Festival renown, graced me with a 2009 big-medicine Christmas gift, a video titled *Peace Through Music*, subtitled "Playing For Change." And it *did* change my life. The director Mark Johnson emphasizes twice in the narration how politics and religion divide us while music is the power that unites us. Again, were I teaching for a living, my students would see this film, along with Petit's *Man On Wire*— no matter the class, be it Intro to Poetry, Intro to Lit, Intro to Cowpoke Cravat Collecting, 101. I agree with *you*, however, that we must buck that "friends don't talk politics or religion" principle, that we must address my reference to "the maestro," at *any* risk. And we will, but not, preferably, as a follow-up to such a joyous poem?

You say "joyous poem," and I immediately think to myself, "So what's new, considering 95 percent of his work is celebratory?" The exceptions being an occasional eulogy or lament—"All This Way for the Short Ride" comes immediately to mind, or, six million times the sorrow, your poem, "Shoes," which arose out of your visit to the Holocaust Museum in D.C. You do write quite a bit out of grief, as did Hugo. And then there's anger—your poem "The Hand," for example. Care to address what seems for you rare, yet extremely effective, poetic catalysts? Grief? Anger? Or, if you prefer, ire?

"Ire" smacks of euphemism. "The Hand" was written out of 200 proof fury—undiluted rage. I was holed up in that old ranch house on Flat Creek south of Augusta, in the foothills below the Rocky Mountain Front. Middle of winter. Late 1980s. Numerically in sync with the wind-chill temps dipping to eighty-something below zero one night. I was all but hugging the wood stove. Had propane as a backup, but in that open country pounded by severe winds, power outages (which would make the propane heaters worthless) were common. My mission, therefore, was to sleep on the couch in the main room with one ear open and to keep the fire banked, as well as the television tuned in to the latest news and weather updates. I might've been watching *Nightline* or some other late-night news magazine show—I don't remember for sure. They aired a segment on apartheid, complete with a camera crew on location somewhere in South Africa. What I witnessed—set thousands of miles away in an arid landscape almost two hundred degrees warmer than the climate just outside my window—offended and infuriated me. Despite my physical and emotional distance—my immediate anxiety over the blizzard conditions—I considered the contents of the TV segment as a personal, far more perilous assault on my world. The local station interrupted the programming with a "severe weather warning," which, as I recall, included the information that propane at such-'n'-such a frigid temperature will jell. Insulating the regulator on the tank was highly advisable. Ripley Hugo had given me Dick's immense, heavy, hooded fishing parka after he died, beneath which I could sheathe myself in layer after layer of cotton, wool, silk, goose down, polyurethane, you name it. Thus bundled, I not so much walked as "plodded like an astronaut or deep sea diver," is how I phrased it in a poem titled, "Feeding Horses In Richard Hugo's Fishing Parka."

The thousand gallon propane "pig" was set a mere twenty paces from the back door. I wrapped and lashed with baling twine an old sougan (cowboy's heavy, patched blanket) around the regulator. I'd just eaten my ritual, before-bed bowl of Wheaties while barely fending off the guilt of possibly shorting the horses on their Arctic ration of alfalfa, so it didn't take much self-convincing, as long as I was hazarding the storm, to prod me toward the barn to pour Cody and Buck their late-night Wheaties flakes as well. Halfway there I turned my back to the wind, noted the flicker of light ever-so-slightly visible from the kitchen window, and became mesmerized by the swirling snow quickly filling in my tracks. "I stood there amazed," to borrow a phrase from the "Home on the Range" lyric, until the only tracks remaining were the ones I was standing in. Never before, or since, have I felt so connected to this earth, felt so aware of each breath, of the exchange of carbon dioxide for oxygen in the lung's microscopic capillaries. Never have I felt so alive, as well as felt the significance of *being* so alive. I believe I also experienced for a nano-moment a heightened degree of tranquility in which I could have happily taken my *last* breath, although I could not have exercised that option, thank my luckiest star, because of my need to get back to the house and engage the poem I knew would confront me. If I hadn't just been accosted by the apartheid footage, I probably would have heated and hammered that minus-eighty windchill factor moment into something ornate, joyous, at the poetry forge. (Someday, I'm certain, I *will* write that poem.) Instead, after a couple of hours of fitful sleep, I leapt out of bed, fed the wood stove, boiled some stout joe, and, still seething, wrote the "The Hand," or, I should say, assisted the poem as it wrote itself. I'm living creative proof that anger does have the capacity to impetuously trump joy on the scale of artistic stimulants. The piece is one of three, maybe four, out of my entire repertoire, that did not beg much, if any, revision. I sent it to Wally McRae with a simple inquiry, "Is this a cowboy poem?" He returned the copy bearing his brief reply penciled, with several hundred foot-pound-pressure, into the cellulose of the page; his sixteen agitated, squiggled letters read, "You *Damn* Right It Is."

Your poem prompted Wally, soon after, to write his impassioned poem, "Ol' Proc," about the black horseman he knew as a young boy?

So it would seem, but you'll have to ask Wally that question.

You initially published "The Hand" in your 1995 collection, I Am Not A Cowboy, *then reprinted it eight years later in* Wolf Tracks On The Welcome Mat. *You also recorded it on your first spoken-word CD,* Words Growing Wild, *then offered it again on the 2006 CD,* Collisions Of Reckless Love. *It's evidently a seminal poem for you. The* Words Growing Wild *version is accompanied by Nashville's Mike Henderson on resonator guitar playing a haunting, raucous, Delta blues riff, while the latter recording is solo voce, if you will. Also, the brief preamble, or proem, you wrote for "The Hand" in the booklet to the earlier CD reads, "Triggered by a television news segment, this socio-political anti-apartheid cowboy poem focuses on African-American hands (short for cowhand) everywhere, whether they ride and rope, or not. God Bless Bill Pickett and God especially bless James Byrd, Jr." Because of the postage stamp sporting Bill Pickett's image, let's assume some folks know his western legacy, but James Byrd?*

In October of 2009, President Obama signed into law the first major piece of federal gay rights legislation, which expanded federal hate crimes to include those committed against people because of gender, sexual orientation, gender identity, or disability. If I'm not mistaken, the bill is named for Matthew Shepherd and James Byrd, Jr. whose families joined President Obama at the White House during the signing. Matthew Shepherd was murdered, found tied to a fence, in Wyoming in 1998. The same year, James Byrd, in Texas, was chained by his neck to the back of a pickup truck by three white men who dragged him until beheaded.

Two questions: First, how do the Elko / cowboy audiences respond to "The Hand"? And secondly, how did they respond to the release of the film Brokeback Mountain, *with all of its Wyoming—"The Cowboy State"—connections?*

The poem received a standing ovation at its debut—full auditorium in Elko. On another occasion in small-town Nevada, a listener stormed out, complained that he didn't buy a ticket to be lectured to, and asked for, and received, a refund. After presenting it at the National Storytelling Festival in Jonesburough, Tennessee, years later, a woman approached me and said how she'd witnessed the same television segment, which angered her equally, and how astonished and pleased she was to hear *our* response cast as a cowboy poem. Until then I'd wondered often if I'd dreamt the segment—whether it had been a brain-freeze hallucination or nightmare brought on by the hellacious cold. Both she and I seemed genuinely thrilled by our chance encounter. We gave each other a big hug—I wish now I'd gotten her name. And then there was the response from Mr. Frank Phillips at the Library of Congress reading—sometime in the 1990s as well. He thanked me for "The Hand," and presented his card, which I still have, embossed with the gold seal of the United States. It read, "Court Systems Division—Thurgood Marshall Federal Judicial Building." It just so happened that Mr. Phillips was Bill Pickett's great-grandson. He later sent me a reproduction of the 1930s movie poster, *The Bull-Dogger*, featuring a large portrait—same one used on the postage stamp, I believe—of his great-grandfather. To wrap up this focus, "The Hand" was also printed as a limited-edition letter-pressed broadside by Bob Blesse of the Black Rock

Press, University of Nevada, Reno. Esteemed Nevada artist and dear, dear friend, Jim McCormick, created a powerful, etched image to accompany the piece.

And Brokeback Mountain?

I saw the Ang Lee-directed film, based on the powerful Annie Proulx short story—from her collection, *Close Range*, which I'd read earlier—in a Great Falls theater. The movie played in town for a mere two or three days and the showing Liz and I attended was almost a private screening—maybe ten of us in all. In Elko the year after the film's release, Brokeback jokes were rampant. For whatever reason—maybe out of empathy for a number of gay, devoted Elko fans and volunteers—I took a stand. In the rodeo-theme session no less, I lamented the sick *Brokeback Mountain* jokes I'd heard the past few days since arriving in Elko. I went on to express how difficult the movie was for me, but how I'd found it, especially the closing scene, as poignant a love story as any I'd witnessed over my half-century fascination with film. Or something along those lines. I then declared that undeniably—no matter one's viewpoint and / or sexual preferences— *Brokeback Mountain* was first and foremost a story about friendship, after which I recited one of the most significant rodeo poems of my remuda, "Partner." This time, *not* to a standing ovation, but rather to sparse, polite, tense applause. Filmmaker Jaime Rodriguez— accompanied by Spanish writer-publisher Javier Lucini—debuted this year in Elko a rough cut of Jaime's provocative documentary on the West, *The Cowboys I Know*. It includes footage taken at last year's (2009) Gathering. My recitation of "Partner"—in praise of friendship, as well as in memoriam and in tribute to Heath Ledger for his *Brokeback Mountain* role—contributes, I'm honored to say, to the vision of Jaime and Javier, as well as that of cameraman, Billy Gerard Frank, three gifted artists who offer a critical viewpoint from outside of our culture. To address what I'm guessing is the gist of your one-two punch question, it's probably a safe bet that racism in the cowboy West is not *quite* as prevalent as is homophobia—an assertion that doesn't really offer much to celebrate, does it?

No it doesn't (pause). Long overdue, "The Hand"?

The Hand

In South Africa, a white aristocrat grabs
the hand of an elderly black man
sitting in the dirt on the edge
of a lush crop. The white man
picks the black man's hand up
as if it were a self-serve gasoline nozzle,
pulls it toward a reporter
and mechanically squeezes the wrist
to spread wide the thick callused fingers
and palm. The white man holds his own hand
open side-by-side. "Do you see
the difference?" he asks. "What
does his hand look like to you? How
can you say we are the same?"

"Do you see the difference?" he asks again,
the reporter stunned by what he is hearing,
while the black man sits inanimate,
his working cowboy hand
filling the camera's close-up lens
with a landscape of canyons,
coulees and arroyos, buttes and mesas, mountains
and plains the black man might have ridden,
hands shaped by pistol grip, lariat, and reins,
had he been born of another geography
and time—just another wind-burned hand
of a *cavvy* man, sinew and knuckle,
flesh and blood, pocked, porous, scarred,
and dark as lathered latigo. The hand
alongside the aristocrat's
tissue-paper appendage always reaching to take
even another man's hand, and own it,
and hold it open, because he knows the fist
is as big as a man's heart
and *this* is the difference he fears.

Round 4

If you're up for it, I'd love to open Round 4 with another "triggering subject" scenario or episode in a similar spirit as those surrounding "The Hand" and "Montana Second Hand."

I lived outside of Santa Fe, New Mexico for a bit in the late 1980s—culture-shock, to say the least, for someone beamed-up out of the Midwest with a long layover in Montana. But I love the landscape, love the people, and especially love the food. I experienced a good number of firsts there, among them my first encounter with flamenco, performed by artist Maria Benitez. I was still riding a few broncs, and felt a distinct kinship between Maria's passionate pursuit for the dance-perfected and that of the bucking horse twister. Her performance—the electricity, the panache, the verve, the moxie, the élan, the ardor, the disciplined tempestuousness, the grit, the soulful downpour of two-hundred-proof passion—flipped the switches on my epinephrine pumps to full-tilt. I absorbed the dance—one stomped foot and handclap per pore—into my deepest being, where it has taken up residence for life. Months later, back in Montana and living in that hundred-year-old ranch house, Maria's dance rose to the surface, busted through the cold and ice and into the warmth of the room, where I sat two feet from the wood stove and worked up the first draft of "Flamenca Duende." The title arrived much later, after Gary

Thompson cued me to a Federico Garcia Lorca essay from which I plucked the epigraph, the springboard into the poem:

Flamenca Duende

> "The duende is a power, not a work;
> it is a struggle, not a thought...,
> not a question of ability, but of true,
> living style, of blood, of the most
> ancient culture, of spontaneous creation
> ....It is, in sum, the spirit of the earth."

Not just any hot Latin blood, but the fiery
blood of Maria Benitez—her heart's
whole voltage into each muscle, perfect
choreography of the body's troupe,
500 strong—is not just any passion
but passion a-horseback
full-gallop with gut-stringed, cypress guitars
to the stampede of hand clap, castanets,
laughter and tragic Andalusian wail
cracking the night like lightning
striking Gypsy moons afire.

Into this flamenca's dance goes the faith
of all saints, one poet's soul, vaquero savvy
and toreador grit, predator
frenzy at the taste of blood, plus a shot
of erotica, rage, and mother love.
When the blur of feet mesmerizes me—
holds me in the black bonds between stars—
I miss the gait of her eyes,
and when I follow her face, chin poised
for passage into the meteor storm of rhythms,
I miss the aerial steps of one hand. Yet,
when I focus on that flight,
the mate solos out of the frame—
impossible to track a duet
of acrobatic toucans through a tropical
canopy's kaleidoscopic dance.

But the Spanish, heir to that grace,
cheer her on: *Olé! Maria! Olé!*
and the ruffled grouse drumming
accelerates to cicada chirr, that chain
reaction of ricochets
rippling through the train of her gown,
through her shawl's foot-long fringes
flailing wild as hot wires
in a gale. As she pivots
finger-snap fast, an earring
whiplashed to the stage
flickers to life, ignited
by the charge of its atoms dancing—
dancing to the pulse of passion's lithe flame
burning for Maria
from the molten center of the earth—dancing,
that gold earring dancing, 'til it too burns.

So is the poem's intent to harness the essence of Maria's passion conveyed through her dance?

Don't ask me. Ask *the poem.* As did "The Hand," it wrote most of it itself, without much direction from me. Besides, there are no destinations when writing a poem—creativity rhymes with infinity. I have yet another postscript, however. I saw Maria dance again in 1997. I did so with heavy trepidation. What if my response this time was less pronounced or, far worse, what if it was every bit as profound but made the poem seem anemic? Call me Lucky, because the power of her dance had *not* diminished and—I swear this truth on my sacred Smith-Corona—I came away not wanting to alter a single image or syllable. For a perpetual, punctilious tweaker such as myself, the odds against this are colossal. I spoke with Maria after her performance and she told me that as a young girl she and her mother had lived in Montana for awhile—on one of the Indian Reservations. Try to convince me that "Flamenca Duende" isn't also a cowboy poem.

And then there's your song lyric companion piece, "Maria Benitez," which singer-songwriter John Hollis put a melody to and recorded. You'd agree that, thematically, it's more of a cowboy song than "Flamenca Duende" is a cowboy poem?

I wrote the lyric long after the poem, and seem to recall consciously focusing on that bucking hoss-twister flamenca-dancer kinship I mentioned. The poem chose not to address that—at least not directly—and I trusted the poem's instinct to veer wherever it needed to veer, as well as my instinct to ride along. While composing the lyric, I took more control—albeit control with a hackamore rather than with the potentially more severe spade bit. I just this instant realized how I'm prone to leveraging some control with the lyric, whereas, to the contrary, I've seldom used anything more than a halter and a buck rein with my poetry. I'm partial to giving the poem its head and trying to stick with it through every acrobatic literati-lariati contorted feat it throws my way. All *Equus caballus* metaphors aside, John Hollis was the first musician to field my neophyte attempts at songwriting. He sent a demo cassette, and I'll never forget the elation as I listened for the first time to a musician's melodic interpretation of my lyric narrative. John augmented the chorus with some Spanish, and created a beautiful lilt. Tom Perlman, Jean Prescott, and Justin Bishop of Horse Sense also cut "Maria Benitez," which, as you suggest, most definitely is more of a cowboy story—much varied from the original poem, focusing purely on Maria, on the dance, in a more ethereal, universal vein.

You seem to have written quite a few poems that speak to music or music-makers and / or that employ music imagery. Many of these works surfaced in the past twenty years, since John Hollis turned your lyric into a song. You've spent a lot of time in recording studios, most recently the Cash Cabin Studio with John Carter Cash and Wylie Gustafson, and yet you don't even play an instrument?

No, I don't play, but I did buy a guitar in the late 1970s. Never got much past three chords, which, of course, was all I needed to concoct a few songs. Very trite stuff. I vaguely remember singing the ditties for rodeo partners in a Miles City motel room. They thought I was the next best thing to Willie Himself, but they'd been drinking and I'm sure the tales I was spinning were rodeo-familiar—I was "singing *their* songs," and could do no wrong.

The poetry urge must have possessed the dominant gene, because I dropped the singer-songwriter interest somewhere along the trail for a dozen years.

The "Maria Benitez" lyric revived it?

Not entirely. In October of 1987 I met the renowned Ian Tyson—formerly of 1960s Ian and Sylvia fame. Wally McRae ramrodded a big show at the Alberta Bair Theatre in Billings, and I was on the same bill with Ian, Chris LeDoux, Baxter Black, Wally, and several other fine poets. Joel Bernstein—of University of Montana Rodeo Team advisor notoriety mentioned earlier—had given Ian a copy of *The Make-Up of Ice*. Ian invited me to have breakfast with him the morning after the performance to talk about the possibility of writing songs together.

Is that what triggered your first co-write, "Rodeo Road"?

No, that song germinated years later. As I recall, I took a pathetic shot at several *rhymers*, which understandably didn't inspire Ian enough to even acknowledge his receipt of them. After a long, *long* silence, we reconnected, and co-wrote "Whispering Hope"—the name of the bucking horse I rode to a first-place win at the Cascade, Montana, rodeo in the early 1980s. Ian never did cut the song. I've cherished, however, the demo cassette, which inebriated Ian tossed to inebriated me in a low-rent Missoula motel room. When I toured with Justin Bishop and Richie Lawrence of Horse Sense in the 1990s, we resurrected it, tinkered with the lyric a bit, and performed it on a bunch of stages. It then slipped back out of earshot for a decade until Wylie Gustafson of Wylie & The Wild West and I began collaborating a few years ago. That Missoula motel room cassette somehow miraculously resurfaced. I sent Wylie a copy and it took hold hard with him, except for the last verse, which Ian had left open-ended. I wrote and rewrote and re-rewrote until Wylie and I both gave our nod of approval to a lyric that we hoped would live up to Ian's wonderful melody. Wylie cut it on his *Bucking Horse Moon* album.

Wasn't that the title of your poem? And the companion song co-written with the highly-revered Tom Russell?

You got it. What a magnificent surprise when, out-of-the-blue—as in *blue* norther—one blustery February morning, I answered the phone and heard Tom's baritone voice over his studio speakerphone, **"Tell me what you think of this, Zarzo."** He sang an early take of "Bucking Horse Moon" while I silently wept on my end of the line. We'd just met weeks earlier in Elko. When I swaggered up to him and introduced myself, he responded with the most "So-the-fuck-what?" look and tone I'd *ever* been confronted by. Until, that is, I mentioned having co-written "Rodeo Road" with Tyson—same reaction, this time emphatically doubled in its degree of disinterest. All of which did not deter me from foisting upon the poor, unsuspecting bastard—yes, "bastard!"—a sheaf of poems that I told him he needed to seriously consider transmogrifying into songs, which in turn would leverage us both up a pickup-truck status notch or two on the cowboy West's economic scales. Truth be known, I'd have bet my riggin' bag, my 1971 Monte Carlo, *and* my Smith-Corona Silent-Super that I'd never again hear from Tom. What a morning, what a moment, what a friendship that began with his call. We've since co-written "Eight Bucks and Change" (unrecorded), "Heart Of A Bucking Horse," and "All This Way For The Short Ride," the latter (adapted from a poem by the same title) a tribute to Joe Lear, a bull rider friend killed in the early 1980s at the Diamond Spur Rodeo in Spokane. To answer your question, Wylie took a serious shine to the "Bucking Horse Moon" song, delivered a dulcet vocal, and dubbed it his title cut. Thus the CD sports a trio of co-writes, one each with Ian, Tom, and Wylie. An honor of utmost magnitude.

So it was Tyson who planted the first song-lyric seed and Hollis who harvested the first complete song? And today, twenty years later, you've co-written how many recorded numbers?

I don't know—twenty-five, maybe. I've written at least another twenty-five—some of them light years from "cowboy"—that none of my musician friends have fielded, of which I make deliberate mention here in hopes that Tom Waits or Lucinda Williams finds a copy of *51*, likely in some thrift store, and takes note of these uncut verses. Betsy Hagar made a wonderful record—*Heavens to Betsy*—produced by virtuoso guitarist Rich O'Brien. It includes a full six pack of Zarzyski lyrics to which she lent unique and beautiful melodies. Ian, Tom, Wylie, Don Edwards, Justin Bishop, Robert Shepherd, John Reedy, Greg Keeler, Jim Haynes from Australia, Peter O'Brien from England and David Wilkie and Denise Withnell of Cowboy Celtic have all embraced my lyrics, thanks to the lariati arena, where I rub creative shoulders with such a stellar *wild bunch* of songwriters and musicians. What an otherworldly Star Trekian journey—as much the adventure as showing up in Missoula in the fall of 1973 to study with Dick Hugo. And speaking of the poems again, and to fully address your initial question about "music imagery" or music references in my work, you're right—I've slowly but steadily circled my way in closer and closer to song, ever since my grad school compadre, Quinton Duval, dazzled me with his playing and singing of Hank Williams. Soon thereafter I discovered Chris LeDoux's rodeo songs—bought his first four 8-tracks and cherish them still. Thirty-plus years later, I catch myself every so often singing one of those stories that made my ticker jump-'n'-kick during my bronc-ridin' days—"Bareback Jack," "Copenhagen," "The Bucking Machine," "Tight Levis and Yellow Ribbons." I knew them all by heart back then and, surprisingly, still do. Got to know Chris a bit over the years, too—mostly behind stage rather than behind the chutes. After he hit it big we'd still exchange an occasional letter or bump into each other now and then at some airport. I miss him—loved his spirit, the energy and honesty of his music. He was fifty-six when he died of cancer. I celebrated my fifty-seventh birthday by watching his videos and playing his CDs. I have few regrets, but on the creative front I wish Chris and I could've written one song together. I believe he'd especially like a few that Wylie and I have broke-to-ride the past few years— Rodeo to the Bone," "A Pony Called Love," "Ain't No Life after "Rodeo," "Cryin' Hole Blues," "Ridin' Double Wild," and, most personally, our tribute to him, to his music, "Cravin' 8s." Man, Chris was singing *my* song—a private concert—when he informed the country-'n'-western world that "Even Cowboys Like a Little Rock-'n'-Roll." I cut my teeth on rock, then discovered Hank, Patsy Cline, Johnny Cash, Merle and Willie, then Chris LeDoux, then Ian Tyson, and Tom Russell, who urged me toward Lucinda Williams, Leonard Cohen—"Tower Of Song," most definitely one of the top ten greatest lyrics ever written—Dave Alvin, Liza Gilkyson, Joe Ely, Gretchen Peters, as well as to rediscover Dylan. Tom is also a big-time Tyson fan. I'll never forget how blown away I was my first year in Elko, 1987, listening to Ian sing cuts from *Cowboyography*, a few of which he and Tom co-wrote. Enriched my life, those two virtuosos did. I owe them big for embracing my writing.

You told a revealing Chris LeDoux story from the stage in Cody, Wyoming, a few years ago. Care to share it here?

For whatever reasons—prior to Cody, where I was asked to pay personal homage to Chris during their twenty-fifth anniversary "Empty Saddles" session—I've kept this fairly private. In May of 2003 I received an envelope sporting Chris's letterhead, forwarded via the Augusta post office where I hadn't received mail for years. It arrived during one of my moments of, shall we say, financial embarrassment? The 1950s carnival piggy bank in which I save pennies and the Green Bay Packer helmet bank that my Dad made out of hardwood and in which I save dimes were both on the kitchen table. I was getting ready to cash in their contents, as I was compelled to do once or twice a year when I found myself short of gas, grocery, and barley soup (beer) mazuma. I unfolded the letter and began deciphering Chris's penmanship, while ignoring what appeared to be a check left inside the envelope. The letter was hand-written on yellow notepad. It reads,

Hello Paul,

I'm sorry I never got back to you when you sent the article on Reg Kesler. You're probably wondering what this check is for…I'll tell you! Toby Keith and I were talking a couple of years ago about writing a song together and the title "Rodeo Moon" came to me. I related to Toby my experiences with my wife on the road and the nights of love and laughter and travel, and how that big old moon was like a gentle friend on those rodeo summer nights. Anyway, Toby took the idea, and changed my wife into a barrel racer and wrote the song. So out of respect for you and your poetry, I feel I owe you a part of this good fortune because of the influence "Bucking Horse Moon" must have had on me. I wouldn't feel right if I didn't send you a portion of the royalties I received from this song. Please accept this and I hope you're doing well.

See ya down the road,
Chris.

The check was for $8,000. Eight—still my all-time favorite number in tribute to all those years I lived craving the 8-second spur ride. Yup, "Cravin' 8s." I phoned a half-dozen musician / producer / Nashville friends and asked them what I should do. Each and every one encouraged me to accept the money, although Toby's song lyric had not included one syllable from my poem beyond the word "moon." Folks close to the music biz shake their heads in awe when I tell them the story. Chris had not one smidgen of obligation to pay me a cent of the royalties. I received two more envelopes, each containing checks adorned with yellow sticky notes reading, "Paul, here's some more money! Chris." His wife, Peggy, recently sent another. You want to talk the height, the very pinnacle, of western / cowboy integrity and generosity? There it is. The gesture changed my life on far more significant fronts than solely that of the monetary. I vowed to Chris that I'd spend the rest of my days heeding his cue. Every now and again I send friends-in-need a little dough along with a note assuring them that the money isn't mine, that "I'm just passing it along— *unused*—from a generous friend."

I'd say, in fact, you did—at least, indirectly—co-write a song with Chris LeDoux.

Thanks. That means a lot.

Back to lyrics. Do they ever distract you from what I believe is your primary writing focus, the poetry? Or do the two seemingly very different disciplines share enough common ground? How fine, or wide, is the line between the lyric and the poem, the verse versus the stanza?

Tom Russell emphatically answers your question in a book he edited with Sylvia Tyson. It's titled *And Then I Wrote—The Songwriter Speaks*, a fascinating collection of commentaries by our most prominent musician-lyricists. In his introduction to

Chapter Six, Tom writes, "Many amateur songwriters confuse the ability to write poetry, or be clever with rhyme, with the essence of lyric writing. Many writers quoted below are very specific in their belief that poetry is vastly different from song lyrics. Sammy Cahn said Shakespeare would have been a lousy songwriter.... I've often thought there's a closer kinship between the painter and the songwriter than there is between the poet and the songwriter."

Do you agree with your friend?

I don't *want* to agree. But first, to address your question regarding "distraction." I consider myself a greenhorn lyricist and, at best, a journeyman poet. I know just enough about writing to know just how little I really know—the more I learn and the farther I *reach*, the more I believe, again, in creativity's infinity. I truly do live for those journeys into the unknown, and I don't distinguish, in a hierarchal sense, between time invested into poetry versus time invested into song lyric. Don't most writers dabble in a variety of forms? Hugo wrote essays, as well as a novel. My friend Red Shuttleworth sees himself first and foremost as a poet but he's known success as a playwright and has also written quite a bit of fiction. Wally McRae has all but abandoned his cowboy poetry in favor of the autobiographical essay. His recent collection, *Stick Horses*, offers some of the most touching, emotionally-honest prose ever written about our cowboy West. And Tom is one of the great Renaissance men of our times—songwriter, painter, novelist, essayist, filmmaker, you name it. Any day now he's likely to call from his adobe studio in Canutillo, Texas, and say, "Zarzo, dig this—I'm sitting here with a bottle of Don Julio Blue Agave Reposado, a potter's wheel, and 51 pounds of Juarez bull ring clay I smuggled, in an iguana-hide duffle bag, through customs and over the Santa Fe bridge, under heavy machinegun fire!" I feel the two disciplines I'm working in are made of almost identical DNA helixes even while hailing from planets that are galaxies apart. Sometimes that "line" you speak of feels as thin and invisible as one-pound-test monofilament, while other times I know how a three-legged turtle feels crossing an expressway during rush hour. Can a stanza be put to music and sung like a verse? You bet. But it's the rare, rare exception rather than the rule. Can a verse be recited or read aloud *a cappella* like a stanza? Perhaps even less likely so. But the writer of both is obsessed with image, rhythm, syntax, syllabics, phrasing, and on and on, *line*-by-jagged-*line*, more so than sentence-by-sentence. I've recited on stage, for example, Kevin Blackie Ferrel's "Sonora's Death Row." I bet I could do the same with Tom's "Hurricane Season" or "The Eyes of Roberto Duran" or a dozen other songs he's oh-so-poetically breathed life into on the page. Same goes for a lyric I wrote—"Black Upon Tan"—which David Wilkie put to music and Denise Withnell sings angelically. With "Black Upon Tan" I do repeat the four-line chorus, but just once. I also omit the tag verse. It's the refrain that feels most foreign to my poetic tongue and ear. With many lyrics, the verses and even the bridge, if they include a richness of poetic image and diction, pose little awkwardness when presented as spoken word. You bet, we're talking Dylan-esque. As well as Russell, Tyson, Cohen, Cash, Nelson, Lucinda Williams, Tom Waits, Steve Earle, Springsteen, and a few other "esques." Hey, I wonder if I could recite The Stones' "Sympathy for the Devil" as a poem?

At cowboy poetry festivals? Forget it. "Wild Horses" maybe. But as long as you bring up Mick and Keith, I've always imagined them co-writing in the same room together, melody and lyric informing one another during an organic, if you will, evolution of the song. Doesn't your solo process involve a severe handicap? Have you ever kick-started a song from scratch with a musician— ever experienced the back-'n'-forth, the give-'n'-take, in the same space, the same moment?

Not yet, but I hope to—especially after reading Sting's interview in the January, 2010 issue of *Esquire*: "People send me song lyrics all the time. It's difficult. I'm not sure what they want me to do with them. Looking at lyrics without the music is like looking at a one-legged man." He also said, "Sometimes mediocre poetry becomes incredible song material." And fortunately for me, I've written more than my share of mediocre poetry. Probably the closest I've come to a "give-'n'-take" co-writing scenario involved one of the most exhilarating episodes of my creative life. Singer-songwriter *par excellence* David Wilkie was passing through Great Falls one March on his way home to Alberta when the spring *big one* hit—roads closed, power out, the whole Arctic-blast shitaree. We were faced with two choices: We could either take up luge, which Dave was adamantly against because of the skin-tight, full-body leotard he said would make him look like a haggis, *or* we could eat my dad's canned Lake Superior Coho with slabs of Asiago cheese, rice crackers, and extra hot Giardiniera, alongside chips and guacamole, all washed down with Guinness and Irish whiskey, while playing and listening to music in front of a roaring fireplace blaze. We both cast our votes for the latter. Might have tried for all of ninety seconds to start a song from scratch, as you say, when, during an uncomfortable lull, David tossed a melody he'd composed earlier out into the blue, phantasmagorial ethers between us. It was so lovely, so fresh, and so foreign to my cowboy-song ear. It spoke volumes of soulful sentiment, *without words*. David, loaded and needing to crash, said, "It's yours if you can do anything with it," as he shut his bedroom door. I scribbled a few blurry notes and went to bed. But then, fearing the storm would cease or, worse, we'd run out of Guinness and David would chance the roads north no matter what, I was at my desk two hours later at four a.m. with that tune riding every molecule of air surrounding me.

Again, I'd deemed the melody *not* that of a cowboy song—though I do subscribe to the late great Buck Ramsey's dictum that "a cowboy song is any song a cowboy likes to listen to." I remember tapping my finger on the desk and humming. I'm ashamed to admit that I couldn't tell you the difference between quarter time and twelve-eighths time, if there even is such a thing as twelve-eighths time. I remember coaching myself (to the plaster-shattering rhythms of Dave snoring in the adjacent room): keep it simple for once, Mister Esoteric-ski; simplicity is singful bliss; sweet, simple, lilting images and diction; minimal, light, gliding lines; visualize the cartoon balloon bob-bob-bobbin' along over the notes. All of which finally sunk in deep enough to sweep the heavily-laden literary forces of Newtonian gravitational pull right out from under me. And thus I found myself crooning to a frolicking, lyrical groove. In other words,

> I'm gliding, I'm sliding
> As high as the moon—
> I'm singing this song out of the blue.
>
> Breeze lifting, I'm drifting
> Like a giant balloon—

I'm flying not falling in love with you.

High on the wing
I know why
Angels sing—
'Cause they're dancing on air
Graceful as prayer
Down love's thoroughfare.

I'm soaring, ignoring
Most all of the rules—
I'm singing this song out of the blue.

Regaling, inhaling
Love's sweet molecules—
I'm flying not falling in love with you.

High on the wing
I know why
Skylarks sing—
'Cause their world is the song
That brings on the dawn
Where love can't go wrong.

Clouds billow, down pillow
Starry whirlpools—
I'm flying not falling in love with you.

I'm flying not falling in love with you.
I'm flying not falling in love with you.

Before David left town, we'd nailed "Flying, Not Falling,
In Love with You." David's wife, Denise, sings it with kind of
an *ingénue* soulfulness, which is, I think, precisely fitting to the
song's attitude. She recorded it on her CD, *Rose Petal Pie*. It's
the most flighty, or sprightly, lyric I've written—dictated as such
by the pre-existing melody—and one of my favorite co-writes.
Other musician friends have mentioned sending melodies for me
to festoon with words but none have followed through. Maybe
they don't want me to feel "like *I'm* looking at a one-legged
man." Because so much has to do with the spirit of the moment,

that magical songwriting episode experienced with David might never again work for me. Same goes for the starting-from-scratch process. Ian Tyson and I have approached it a time or two, but didn't get deep enough in to qualify as a Mick-and-Keith effort. I wrote the lyric to "Jerry Ambler" and sat in Ian's stone house, where he holds his Muse hostage when She's agreeable, while he experimented with melodies and prodded me toward a restructuring of the lyric. I resisted—thank goodness for dumb instinct. The first time I heard his "white-bread-rap" arrangement of the song, he was on stage at the Monterey Cowboy Poetry and Music Festival—kind of a "take it or leave it" situation. Even if the audience hadn't responded with revel, I'd have gotten down on a knee and kissed Ian's ring in gratitude for his willingness to trust, to run with, the original lyric I pitched him. What a *reach*! He's the most *F*earless artist in the ranahan arena.

Earlier, I let the word slide in a poem you recited..."ranahan?"

Old term for "top-hand cowpuncher."

So to sum up, you became enchanted, after fifteen to twenty years of writing primarily poetry, with a form, with a discipline, that you feel is commensurate in structure, in technique, yet offers an almost entirely fresh set of challenges, including your earlier nemeses, strict meter and rhyme?

Strict meter? I hear words like "phrasing" and "singability" from my co-writers. I catch myself tapping out syllabic counts against a thigh or the desktop. As for the rhyme, I've fallen for it hard—so hard that Ian, Tom, and Wylie have urged me to back off, to employ more blank verse or slant rhyme. Beyond form, what I've come to realize is that I'm again enthusiastic about rodeo subject matter, which I've seldom been drawn to since the publication of *All This Way For The Short Ride* in 1996. I was convinced I'd said everything I had to say about my bucking horse passion. But the song lyric has opened doors to subject matters, to sentiments and sensibilities, that I had either worn thin in poetic form or had not been able to engage at all. I hope I've never written a poem that doesn't roll out the heavy, embossed **"Imagination Welcomed!"** red carpet. I *know* I've never written a lyric that doesn't do so. And I'm especially pleased with the work

Wylie and I cut on the John Carter Cash production, *Hang-n-Rattle!*

You wrote seven of the thirteen lyrics on Hang-n-Rattle!, as well as the hidden-track recitation, "Bob Dylan Bronc Song." Out of that 8-pack (your lucky 8 again) all but one, "Grace," highlight rodeo themes. Can you further elaborate on the rodeo reinvigoration point?

Wylie resuscitated my bucking horse addiction when he put a rock-n-*rowel*, "Honky Tonk Women" riff-echo to a poem I wrote almost two decades ago, "Ain't No Life After Rodeo." Resuscitated, hell—he plastique-blasted the flood gates off their rusted-shut hinges. The demo disk he sent got my youth juices rushing so torrentially, I foolishly considered cracking back out on the senior rodeo circuit. I warned Wylie that he'd have to live with the guilt of having been an accessory to my suicide. All absurdity aside, I realized later that Wylie's timing, his prodding me back toward strengths I exercised in my rodeo days, helped me to weather the turmoil in my head and heart over Dad's dire illness. The CD liner note I wrote speaks to how our creative endeavor together became the critical, emotional underpinning to one of the most agonizing episodes of my life.

> *Hang-n-Rattle!* Bear down! Cowboy up! Try! Charge hard! "Did you come to hide, or did you come to ride!": to *ride*, with heart, your work, your journey, your trek, your quest, your time here on earth. Grit it out! Dig deep! **Endure!** Metaphorically speaking, we titled this remuda of songs with a human, universal mantra and mandate. In fact, Wylie and I strived to practice precisely what the title preaches while we spurred the words together over a 10-month span in 2008. During the same time, it's no small coincidence perhaps that I was encouraging my beloved, extremely ill father to hang tough— "Do not go gentle into that good night. Rage, rage against the dying of the light." To regain his health, Dad reached deeper than any cowboy, hanging and rattling in the middle of an impossible bronc ride, ever reached way down

inside himself to make it to the welcome whistle. I, on the other hand, felt helpless. All I could do— thanks to Wylie beckoning me toward the healing powers of the creative spirit—was to faithfully kneel and pray my lyrics ("…our daily poem, our prayer") at the holy threshold of Leonard Cohen's "Tower of Song."

Leonard Zarzyski died on October 10. I saw to it that "Knocking on Heaven's Door" was included in the hymns sung from the choir loft during the service at St. Mary's Church in Hurley, Wisconsin, a hundred or so crow-flown miles from Bob Dylan's childhood home ground. My Dad loved to fish and, thus, I also magically planted a symbolic "trout" in the most light-hearted lyric of this cowboy album—a blues lyric, no less. Writing these songs, along with our spiritful recording of them, a month after my dad's passing, with John Carter Cash at the Cash Cabin Studio graced with the sacred memorabilia and memories—with the very presence—of *his* dad, offered a colossal poultice, an anodyne applied to my anguished soul. For this blessing of friendship beamed down lovingly from the Musical Universe, thank you, Brother Wylie.

Although this might seem to you like an odd digression, a far-fetched reminiscence, I couldn't help, while listening to your sentiments of friendship and loss, but to think of Susanna Clark's liner notes paean in the CD titled Poet: A Tribute to Townes Van Zandt. *Do you know the CD? Do you know about Guy and Susanna's long friendship with Townes? Seems to me you'd be a big fan of his lyrics.*

I actually read Susanna's liner notes over the air—it moved me so deeply—a few years back during a radio interview. Here's just a snippet: "We'd talk about the language and words and poetry and songs. More often than not he'd read me his new poem of the day. *Songs always had to work as a poem on paper first.* Townes' rule." And, since we're talking Townes, in the documentary, *Be Here To Love Me*—filmed in part during his waning days—when an interviewer asked him if he had any remaining goals or aspirations, Van Zandt, seemingly in a haze, replied, "...yeah, I'd like to write some songs, you know, that are so good nobody understands them, not even me." I stood in my living room and applauded. When I relate that exchange to fellow writers, however, few seem to get it. As fewer yet, I'm sure, get the metaphorical significance of the photograph, taken by my producer friend Gordon Stevens on the back of our spoken-word CD, *Collisions Of Reckless Love*—me, grinning, my cowboy-booted right foot pressing down the bottom three strands of a barbed wire fence while I'm lifting, stretching, the top two strands upward with my right hand and, with the left spread open and extended behind me toward Hubble images of the cosmos, inviting all writers, all artists, to duck through the fence, to step out of the compromised, cloistered, and complacent—the dissected and defined—conformist comfort zones that fetter us all, and to participate in creativity's most infinite *reaches*.

I think you've addressed clearly how lyric-writing has afforded you a re-ride of the rodeo theme you felt you'd ridden to a stand-still. Has the lyric offered you entrée to subject matters or points of view that you'd seldom approached via your poems?

I believe it has and I owe that revelation to Betsy Hagar, with whom, as I mentioned earlier, I co-wrote six songs on her CD, *Heavens To Betsy*. At least three of those six cuts speak from a woman's perspective or sensibility. As I intimated earlier while describing my childhood environment, men became men by passing tests of physical endurance. In his eightieth year, my dad reported how he'd trudged up, without resting, a long, extremely-steep trail after fishing the mouth of the Montreal River, and how he felt that feat earned him "another year." I told you the story about him attempting to surgically remove a fish hook, sans anesthetic. While in the navy, decades earlier, after a fifth of whiskey, he removed a plantar wart—half an inch deep, he told me—with his pocket knife. Yes, we're talking that old-school, macho resistance to pain, to discomfort, to going soft. In his waning days, my dad was still putting in twelve-hour shifts at the hardware store. Fretting that the manager, my high school classmate Greg Loreti, kept Dad on the payroll out of deference to our friendship, I made it clear that neither I nor my father would take it personally if Greg filled the position with a younger worker raising a family and more in need of the income. "I'd be glad to lay the stubborn Polack off," Gregory responded, "but then I'd have to hire three twenty-five-year-olds to do the work he does." Not only my dad but pretty much every hematite-hearted, red-blooded, rural Wisconsin north-woods male I grew up with exhibited the same grit. It didn't matter that I felt greater kinship, in many ways, with my mother's more sensitive pedigree. All to say, I've spent my life coercing the dominant feminine humors to take a back seat to my far more recessive masculine juices. I've *succeeded*, for better or worse, thanks to the personas I've staked my claim to: hunter, football player, weightlifter, beer-hall brawler, motorcycle outlaw, hard drinker, packer of hod, tripper of timber, and lifter of everything heavy, roughstock rider, enthusiast of the sweet science, writer of rock-n-rowel poetry and song, and on and on. What a relief and epiphany both to discover and bring to the surface the strong-woman sensibilities in the songs I wrote with Betsy, as well as in a number of other lyrics, including the outrageous "Ms. of the Mega-Munitions," triggered by a single line delivered by one of the most spirited elder poets to ever grace our cowboy bard tribe, Alice Schumacher. She was well into her eighties when I visited her home a decade or so ago here in Great Falls. Brought along a sixer of microbrew stouts and porters which, being German, she imbibed with great delight. Unfortunately, some sphincter-of-the-umpteenth-pucker had recently abducted her beloved schnauzer out of her fenced backyard. She was heartbroken, and the heartbreak was both palpable and contagious. I must've asked her if she felt safe there alone after such a brutal intrusion. "I got a shotgun under the love seat," was her affirmative, and that was the seed from which germinated my most hyperbolic writing ever. Get a *load* of this:

> She's got a shotgun under the loveseat
> A Colt .45 in each drawer
> A derringer tucked in her garter belt
> Her boudoir is warrior décor
> Her mattress is literally ticking
> Her bedposts are Tomahawk rockets
> There's an Uzi beneath every pillow
> She's got walk-in ammo closets.

Torpedoes are stacked in the bathtub
There's a blow-gun that's made from a bone
A crossbow is cocked near the toilet
And her flamethrower looks like a phone
She's got hot nitroglycerine faucets
And bandoliers festoon each room
There's a land mine under the WELCOME mat
Ring the bell, bah-dah-bing, bah-dah-BOOM!

    She's the Ms. of the Mega-munitions
    She's sweet vigilante law
    She's a Bonnie Parker arsenal
    In *femme fatale* Shangri-la
    The heiress to the hair-trigger
    Bouncing Betty of Viet Nam
    She's feminine armageddon
    She's the Bombshell with the Bomb.

Her vestibule's filled with bazookas
There are mortars galore on her porch
A nuke submarine in her basement
Her powder room light is a torch
There are ack-ack guns in her attic
A Sherman tank parked in her garage
Her pantry could pass for a battleship
Bon appetit and *bon voyage.*

The C-4 is stored in her parlor
Big Bertha is perched in her den
The smart bombs she keeps in her mezzanine
In the mudroom, dumdums for men
With her atrium Minuteman silo
And her rooftop, a Cobra jet pad
With her B-52-cockpit greenhouse
She's the **last** gal you want to make mad!

    She's the Ms. of the Mega-munitions
    She's sweet vigilante law
    She's a Bonnie Parker arsenal
    In *femme fatale* Shangri-la
    The heiress to the hair-trigger

Bouncing Betty of Viet Nam
She's feminine armageddon
She's the Bombshell with the Bomb.

She's a Bonnie Parker arsenal
In *femme fatale* Shangri-la.

Did you ever show this to your friend Alice?

I didn't finish it in time to share it with Alice before she passed—I think she'd have chuckled a bunch, especially after a few microbrews.

"Ms. of the Mega-Munitions" aside, your lyrics in praise of strong women involve mostly serious focuses—"No Forbidden Flowers," perhaps the best example. But why did it take the lyric to bring this sensibility out in you—why not the poem?

I admit it's taken me a while to cast powerful feminine roles in my poetry, but I do think I at least approached such sensibilities— mostly via celebration of, and empathy for, women—in poems such as "The Garnet Moon," "Flamenca Duende," "Sister Sundays," and, on a lighter note, "Escorting Grammy to the Pot-Luck Rocky Mountain Oyster Feed at Bowman's Corner." Also, albeit less *head-on*, in "Bucks in Rut" and "I Believe." And then, perhaps most directly, in "I Thought That Hope *Was* Home," dedicated to a dear artist friend, Sally Brock: "Tree ring, trout stream, / circle and swirl all know this world / was still miracle before words, / but the world before woman was mere / rock, water, wood, dark."

So to sum up, to close the book on this subject, 1) you believe a blood-sisterhood exists between the poetic stanza and the lyric verse, and 2) you believe, thanks to your song-writing endeavors, you've been afforded entrée to creative dimensions heretofore unexplored?

Guilty as charged on both counts. Writing lyrics has most definitely expanded my creative vistas. But I have an ulterior motive, most succinctly expressed in Guy Clark's song, *Cold Dog Soup and Rainbow Pie:*

Ain't no money in poetry
That's what sets the poet free
And I've had all the freedom
I can stand.

But you have, in fact, managed to make a life, if not a living, on the wages of poetry, haven't you? And miraculously without having to hold down a steady teaching position?

It would take hours to speak comprehensively to my attitudes concerning the classroom. The short of it goes something like this: As a grad student with a teaching assistantship, I feebly taught English composition to freshmen. Later I taught technical writing in the forestry department. I tried to encourage students to think, to tap into their creative cells, to narrow the gap between the sciences and the arts. I cross trails with one of those forestry employees now and then and they often sing the class's praises, which honors me immensely. Next, in the early 1980s, I found myself substituting for Dick Hugo. I'd been working as a timber faller and, believe me, after that experience I'm lucky to be alive. I'd maniacally flail away with my full-throttled Husqvarna while hung-up "widow makers," breaking loose from their cross-locked crowns, crashed down around me. Any day I was off the job because of weather or equipment breakdowns was like a death row reprieve from my self-execution. Had I been employed north of the Medicine Line, I'd have been known in the timber industry as "Zed Man Walking!" Merrell Clubb, English Department Chair, phoned me on one of those reprieves. I was home and up to my elbows in chainsaw parts. He asked if I'd be interested in teaching Dick's scheduled classes while he was recovering from surgery, hospitalized in Seattle—asked if I could meet him in his office immediately to discuss the possibility. I distinctly remember Mr. Clubb apologizing that he could pay me merely $7500 per quarter—for twelve weeks of teaching. At age thirty I'd not earned that much income in a full year. I jumped at the chance to get out of the trees—to maybe live another twelve weeks—especially with winter coming on, and inquired as to how much prep-time I had before classes began. He looked at his watch and said, "If you hurry upstairs to room 320...."

210

It would stand to reason that students who were looking forward to studying with such an icon might've been somewhat chagrined when you walked in instead of Hugo—how were you received?

I'm sure they were disappointed, but I remember being received with compassion and understanding, especially by one of the older students, Verlena Orr, with whom I've remained friends for thirty years—what a brilliant poet she became, *despite* having me for an instructor. I taught for two quarters, in the midst of which Hugo died. I taught briefly again during the winter of 1987. I'd just ridden my last Montana Pro-Rodeo Circuit Finals in Great Falls. "Out of chute number six, on the National Finals horse Whiskey Talks, Professor Paul Zarzyski...." Then, two weeks later, I entered-up in my first National Cowboy Poetry Gathering. Walking out onto the main stage in Elko's Convention Center Auditorium, I heard, "Our next poet, representing Montana, from Missoula...."

So your last steady teaching employment was in 1987, almost twenty-five years ago?

My last steady *any* employment, I guess I should be ashamed to admit. Although there have been lots of "visiting / hit man lecturer" gigs. For the past six or eight Octobers I've joined esteemed writer, photographer, visual artist, and theater friends at the Hobble Diamond Ranch just east of Big Timber. We engage students from a trio of private academies in Pennsylvania united with students from several Montana high schools. Our classrooms include bunkhouses, the cook shack, the horse barn, and cottonwood groves on the banks of the Yellowstone River. No florescent lights, no buzzers between classes, little regimentation. A teaching and, for me, a learning experience I celebrate—thanks to the vision, wisdom, and generosity of the proprietors of the ranch, Bob and Susan Burch, who kicked it all off and continue to make it happen.

What about the Johnston Center for Integrative Studies at the University of Redlands, in California?

Yes—with its most innovative faculty and bright, ambitious students creating a teaching environment in which I absolutely thrive. Thanks to my professor-friend, Kathy Ogren—whom I met, not so incidentally, because of her interest in cowboy poetry—my mission, for fifteen consecutive years now, has been to infuse poetry into classes titled, for example, "Jazz and Blues Literature," "Philosophy Of Religion," "Music and Social Change," "Seduction of the Innocent—Comics, Graphic Novels, and Sequential Art," "The Sixties," "Animal Ethics," "Food and Gender," you name it. In March of 2009, while working my ritual four-day residency, I agreed, at the request of one of Kathy's colleagues, Dr. Jennifer Tilton, to attend a trio of classes at a high-security, juvenile correctional facility. We're talking teenagers, many cuffed, some maybe sedated, and all in institutional garb. Mostly young men, as I recall—mostly blacks and Hispanics. I stood before them in my cowboy clothes and talked poetry. Aside from perusing a few samples of their writing, I didn't have time to get much of a glimpse into the lives of these inmates—where they came from, less so than where they were going. I knew I had a mere seventy to eighty minutes with each group, each so-called "class." Where do you begin? How can you hope to establish, in such little time, in light of such immense cultural chasms, even a thin connective thread? What *was* immediately obvious in their faces, however, was far more sorrow than anger—maybe even far more goodness than evil. I've not been able to talk much about that day's encounters. But *because* of the rapport I'd experienced the preceding October with the Hobble Diamond Ranch high schoolers, who danced around my car as I played for them Wylie singing "Ain't No Life After Rodeo," and *because* they gifted me, in return, with several burned CDs of their favorite rap and hip-hop artists, and *because* I played those discs driving the two hundred miles back to Great Falls late at night, played them at high volume mostly to stay awake but also to understand a bit what makes those students tick, and *because* one cut in particular, titled "99 Problems," by rap artist Jay-Z (you bet, a fellow **Z**) tickled me during a *Bizarzyski* moment with the extremely amusing, albeit extremely politically-incorrect refrain, "If you're having girl problems, I feel sorry for you son / I got ninety-nine problems but a bitch ain't one...HIT ME!" and *because*, lastly, that line surfaced while doing my cowboy poet show for those young inmates and it tickled *them* that I not only knew the Jay Z refrain but dug it enough to be able to deliver it with attitude, we miraculously bonded enough to laugh *with* one another, to give one another nods of coolness approval. Never before had I seen such a speed-of-light narrowing of the sociological and generational gap—thanks to all those connected cosmic dots which led to two little lyrical rap lines transmuting into a huge bridge. I walked out of that facility after engaging my last and most-hardened group of inmates—one or two already sentenced to life, I was told—and almost dropped to my knees, completely spent, beyond exhausted, nothing physically, mentally, spiritually left. It was very likely the most soul-centering, heart-wrenching, mind-altering, disarming, and humbling interaction I will ever know as a teacher.

Would you revisit the institution, the experience?

I honestly don't know that I could, not without risking irreparable transmogrification to my psyche, which isn't all that healthy to begin with, you no-doubt have discerned by now. I worked with middle school teachers during my Montana Arts Council, visiting-poet years. I can't even begin to imagine five shifts *that* arduous per week, eight to nine months per year, twenty-five to thirty-five years per lifetime. And now just try to transcribe that intensity, that responsibility, to what those instructors at the juvenile correctional institutions encounter day-after-day. If I'd had to return the following morning, I'd have collapsed going through the metal detector.

So almost forty years after your graduate student teaching assistantship duties, you bring the bacon home today as a presenter on stage in front of a paying audience rather than as a presenter in front of a classroom.

Yes, thank goodness for Horace Greeley's advice—"Go West, young man, go West,"—enduring 101 years after his death in 1872 and ringing true to me in 1973; thank goodness for Richard Hugo and the University of Montana Creative Writing Program, for the dozen other mentors I met up with on that campus, including Quinton Duval, Gary Thompson, and my rodeo partner and longtime guru Kim Zupan who, more than anyone else, kept my roughstock fires burning hot; thank goodness for yet another mentor and role model, Wallace McRae, the sagebrush sage of Rosebud Creek and puncher-poet extraordinaire; thank goodness for his compadre and, later, mine, Mike Korn, Montana's State Folklorist in the 1980s, who, together with Wally, conspired to introduce this Roughie Free-verser to the hallowed stages of the daddy of 'em all in Elko; thank goodness, *especially*, for the Western Folklife Center, its blue-ribbon crew of visionaries (including, in the Gathering's formative stages, New Mexico's Elizabeth Dear, who's become the love of my life these past twenty-three years), who deemed my work worthy of repping for such a rich legacy and culture; thank goodness for the thousands of fans and fellow artists alike, with whom I've spurred the words wild, with whom I've become friends and co-writers and collaborators; thank goodness for the Wild West with its Wild, wide-open spaces inhabited by Wild beings of wide diversity, from the cowboy to the cougar, from the Indian to the silvertip grizzly, from the marmot to the magpie to the mule deer to the meadowlark, the wild iris and wild rose, the western Muses: "Oh give me a home where the *Poetry* roams."

And Paul Zarzyski?

It's so much less about me than it is about those entities and influences I've just paid tribute to. I'm just a fly-speck in the black-and-white, 8-by-10 *light year* (not inch) glossy of the universe's cast of creative players, the Creator, Him or Her or Itself, front-row-center. I'm just a single miniscule dot, fortunate enough (yup, more dumb luck) to be connected to the 51 nonillion single miniscule dots composing the proverbial Big Picture. An immense, 1950s "Cowboy Cosmos" kid's coloring book, if you will.

To quote Joe Cocker at Woodstock, you "get by with a little help from your friends"?

Absolutely. In fact, I've intentionally saluted these friends by naming many—though, unfortunately, not all—throughout this interview. I look forward to seeing their names in print, despite the risk of reader disinterest. I spoke to my adamant slant on this note in the *Big Sky Journal*'s 2002 Arts Issue, a piece I titled "Montana Flashbacks: A Poetic Toast to Friendship," in which I proclaim the erroneous wording of that old saw, "You are what you eat." I suggest instead that, "We are who we *meet*." And I've met and have been befriended by thousands of kindred travelers, a good percentage of these fellow beings not even belonging to our genus and species, I should add. Since the spring of 1972, since enrolling in David Steingass's Intro to Poetry Writing class at the University of Wisconsin—Stevens Point, my passion for *ars poetica* has acted as catalyst for the majority of these chance encounters of the strike-it-rich kind. *Call Me Lucky*, also—though to some it might seem a facetious stretch—to have been born a Zarzyski, alphabetical brethren Zed-man to the likes of Zevon, Zappa, Zimmer, Zapata, Zupan, ZZ Top, and Emile Zola, the French novelist and critic who declared, "I am here to live out loud." I'll go so far to as to exercise alphabetical anarchy and include Van Zandt, both Townes and Steve. As well as Zorro and Zozobra. Zarzyski (Zarzecki), by the way, means "people from the other side of the river."

I'm anxious to discuss your love for animals or, as you referred to them several sentences ago, "fellow beings." Help me make sure we don't lose track of that focus in the next round. Taking precedence, however, your reference to "the Creator" with its allusion to, I think, something far more eternal than what we celebrate here on earth. Didn't you take this on, metaphorically, in a long essay you wrote for your painter friend Walter Piehl's retrospective catalog?

You're the first to acknowledge the existence of that piece since I wrote it back in ought-three, I believe. Is this the passage you're referring to?

> Somewhere out in the cosmos, in some other dimension, exists this glorious crossroads (call it "Heaven," if you wish) where artists of all disciplines, of all designations—"folk" to "fine" to "funk" to friggin whatever we've so feebly labeled them—gather at some clapboard-humble roadhouse or speak-easy or juke joint. I picture it an amalgamation of the Cotton Club, the Savoy, Carnegie Hall and the Grand Ole Opry. If you find yourself suddenly in that magical place, you know you belong there, it's as simple as that— no applications, certifications, confirmations, qualifications, or any other *-ations*. Moreover,

you've already checked your ego at the door without directions or orders to do so. As my mentor, poet Richard Hugo, insisted…"there are no rules; well, just one—don't be boring." Hugo, by the way—should you find yourself at this beauty-'n'-truth nucleus of the universe crossroads—owns the '62 Buick convertible parked right up front.

One more excerpt to sound the closing bell to this round?

How's this?

…You bet, the walls are covered with art, with poems, and photographs and memorabilia. One wall is a bookshelf far as the eye can see…I imagine a Walter Piehl painting shoulder-to-broad-shoulder with a Jackson Pollock on one side and a Willem De Kooning on the other. There are a thousand stages, a thousand and one dance floors, opera to ballet, big band to rap, Shakespeare to cinema—you name it, if it's art, it's here, along with all the creators through all of time, God included, though you can't tell God apart from the other Makers, the other Givers-of-Life, as God was the very first to check God's ego at the swinging doors.

Round 5

You've referenced the Creator and God, and it sounds as though you're a believer in some kind of master plan or next dimension. But you take pokes and potshots at religion in two or three poems printed in Wolf Tracks On The Welcome Mat *and more recently in your poem, "Good Friday," written after your dad's passing. Please speak to your spiritualism or spirituality.*

Spirituality, religion—they're just words with nebulous definitions. And, yes, I admit taking offense with, and attacking, the latter, especially because it's become impossible for me personally to hear or see the term without its nefarious, insidious accompanying modifier—*organized* religion. Rather than an abstract rant, however, I'd like to relate a personal experience to elucidate what cues me to a belief—faith, maybe—that Something is out there. In the early 1990s, after turning forty and riding another twenty-five or thirty broncs on the senior rodeo circuit, I wrote a poem titled "Benny Reynolds' Bareback Riggin'." Benny won the World Champion All-Around Cowboy title in 1961, was still riding roughstock in his late fifties, and was still using what was likely the only bareback riggin' he'd ever owned—talk about a handicap— to out-ride us youngsters in our early forties. Anyway, Liz and I were passing through Dillon, Montana, on our way to Santa Fe, and stopped at a trading post operated by a grand old cowboy, Tex Smith, a friend of Benny's. Tex had an antique—1940s or 1950s—riggin' for sale, which I dubbed the perfect stage prop for the poem I'd written. He wanted $35.00 for it, more than fair, but it's the cowboy way to dicker. I told him about my intentions, and he asked me to recite the poem. It tickled him so much that he made the counter-offer of the century: "If you'll give me $17.50, I'll kick in the other half." My end of the bargain had a favor tacked on to it, however. Jerry Ambler—World Champion Saddle Bronc Rider, 1946—had been killed in a car wreck outside of Monticello, Utah, in 1958. He supposedly died broke and alone, so his rodeo buddies pitched in to buy a tombstone. Tex had never been to the grave and asked us if we'd pull into the cemetery and let him know if a marker had in fact been erected. We found the site, took pictures of the classy marble, and sent him the snapshots. I've been known to deem the invention of death as "the gravest (yes, pun intended) fault in God's design,"—likely the aftermath of a cheap tequila hangover, before God conceived of reposado, 100 percent agave azul. Which is to say, I'm not at all fond of cemeteries, of death in general, it's no secret to anyone who's read my work, especially of late. Thus it surprised the bejeezus out of me how comfortable I felt in that setting. For luck, I kept a Kennedy (another of my personal heroes) fifty-cent piece in the watch pocket of my Wranglers, and I slipped it down between the base of the tombstone and the turf that had shrunk away from it in the summer drought.

Not long afterwards I wrote a free-verse poem and the song lyric, the latter first, which is unusual for me, both titled simply, "Jerry Ambler." Few people know the poem, but Ian Tyson brought notoriety to the lyric, as I've touched on earlier, with the unique riff he applied. The song triggered curiosity in, and research into, Ambler's wild-bunch, rodeo-rounder life. (Rumor has it, there's both a book and movie in the works.) Ian and I have heard tale-after-pilgrimage-tale of folks stopping by the gravesite—paying homage by leaving small mementos, including, Ian was told, a copy of the CD, *Ian Tyson, Live At Longview*, on which the song is recorded.

I'm reluctant to tell you this, but I felt a presence—unlike any I've ever experienced—during that initial visit, and have felt it again and again, to varying degrees, during subsequent stops. I'm sure the setting itself has more than a skosh to do with it. You bet, mountains, grass, sky, but far beyond the bucolic visual—the obvious western symbols—something about the air, about every venerable breath I breathe while in the presence of that stone, places me in the most quintessential cowboy West I've known, deeper even than those winning bucking horse rides took me. *My* experience, however, is not the essence of the story. In the spring of 2008, I found the following message—transcribed here verbatim—on my voice mail: "Paul? This is Joyce Feeley. I'm from Cody, Wyoming. And we're down by Monticello, Utah. And we lost our son in a car accident. He was a saddle bronc rider. And we want to visit the place that you wrote the poem about that Ian Tyson sings. And we're not exactly sure where it is, but we'd like to talk to you about it because we're on our way there to visit the site. Because we think our son wants to talk to us from there."

I was home to answer the phone several weeks later when Mr. Feeley called. He told me that his son Cort was killed on Halloween night the year before (2007). Cort had been a good saddle bronc rider, an outfitter, an all-around athlete, and, it was obvious, his dad's best friend. Bill emphasized right off that he was not some religious fanatic, but he felt a need to share with me a "spiritual moment" he'd experienced because of the song Ian and I had written. He recounted how he'd found himself drawn to the crash site, "seven miles up South Fork," again and again, in search of something, anything, to offer solace, some "sign," some "answer," I think were his words. One Sunday, after seeing a young father and his son fishing, Bill was overcome with the feeling that Cort wanted to tell or show him something. He made another pilgrimage up South Fork and, while walking the same ground he'd walked numerous times before, he looked down and saw a disc, a shiny silver disc, cracked, weathered, and muddy. Yes, thrown from his son's vehicle six months earlier. Ian Tyson's *Live at Longview* CD. He took it home and put it in the player. "Jerry Ambler" was one of the few audible tracks—complete with Ian's gracious praise for my lyric as an introduction to the song. Bill immediately identified the otherworldly connections to his son's life and fate. He believed it offered that sign he was seeking. Unbeknownst to Bill, however, his wife Joyce had already— *before* he'd found the disc and discovered the Ambler song set in Monticello, Utah—made plans to drive to Moab to rendezvous with her sister and brother-in-law. Bill told me how hard he and Joyce had been taking their loss, how they desperately needed a change of scenery. He checked the road atlas, realized they'd be a mere 51 miles north of Monticello once they'd reached Moab, and he packed the disc. He related how they'd gone to the sheriff's department to get directions to the cemetery, how they found the grave on the cemetery chart, how he walked up to the marker, placed his hand upon it and felt his son Cort assuring him, "I'm okay, Dad—don't worry, Jerry's taking care of me."

"It saved my life, Paul," he said, "and I want to thank you and Ian for writing that song."

What a beautifully moving story—but I'm not entirely clear where you're going with it, what the point is?

For me personally, life's ultimate mission is far less about discovering and adhering to the man-made tenets of a conforming, congruent, organized religion than it is about witnessing, as keenly as humanly possible, the otherworldly encounters of my own one-of-a-kind-in-all-of-time life. I truly believe this to be the divine intention—to bear great enough witness to the gift of one's own existence. *It*, in turn, may then open the heart, the mind, and, yes, the spirit, to receiving the freedom and wisdom, and perhaps faith, with which to acknowledge and celebrate the existence of the entire living fabric. Most succinctly, my primary challenge is to learn to explore the mysteries from my very own unique vantage point in this miraculous universe—granted, no small *non*-existential feat. Yes, my personal ethos feels antithetical to the motivation of most religions, which is conformity—to coerce each member of the congregation *not* to think individually, but rather to act, and to react, precisely alike, as a whole, as a single entity, in accordance with some folkloric / fairy tale-ish / mythological "book of rewards and punishments." Although I'm interested in the possibility of other dimensions or parallel universes or whatever you want to call the afterlife—for me, most certainly something other than warring heaven and hell—I can't help but to subscribe to the philosophy of the Roman poet known as Decimus Junius Juvenalis (A.D. 60?-140): "It is sheer madness to live in want in order to be wealthy when you die." I got a double sawbuck that says ol' Juvenal ain't eternally burning as we speak. My ideologies aside, what rises with clarity and vehemence from between the lines of the Jerry Ambler / Feeley family encounter is the power of creativity. Ponder the sequence of events with me. How so many *exact*—appointed or designated, but not "chosen," goddamnit—people had to be in the *exact* place together at precisely the *exact* moments in time with precisely the *exact* synergistic, synchronistic, spiritual and philosophical and emotional focuses *and* forces....

...as in, Paul Zarzyski meets David Steingass (poetry) meets Richard Hugo (University of Montana) meets Kim Zupan (rodeo) and Wally McRae (cowboy poetry) and Ian Tyson (cowboy song) meets Elizabeth Dear (New Mexico) meets Benny Reynolds meets Tex Smith meets Jerry Amber (a trio of old rodeo top hands) meets Joyce and Bill and Cort Feeley (fellow human being westerners to the core) meets . . .

Bingo! All of the above liaisons fueled by that one stimulating nexus, that single creative light empowering us as vehicles or conduits or pony express relayers whose *exact* thoughts and actions become responsible for, in this case, a grieving man's hand being placed upon the gravestone of a bronc rider killed in a car wreck almost a half-century before the grieving man's bronc rider son was also killed in a car wreck. But...what was the question again?

I think it was whether or not you "subscribe to a spirituality" or "spiritualism," of sorts?

I hope so. I think I do. Yes—sans organized religion, in no small part because, number one, I believe in an *egoless* supreme being, and two, even if God was experiencing a rare moment of insecurity and decided, "I might feel a whole lot better about what I am and what I've created if only I had a fan club," would you, were you God, choose the inferior likes of *us* as the members who'll cheer you on? I sure as hell wouldn't. Especially in light of how religions, a.k.a. fan clubs, or cults, have been responsible throughout history—arguably never more so than today— for some of the world's most heinous acts against humanity, against the Creator's beloved planet earth and its occupants. Merely in recent times, consider the missionaries' crimes against indigenous peoples and the atrocities committed by pedophile Catholic priests and Muslim suicide terrorists crashing planes full of people into buildings full of people, in order to earn in the afterlife eternities full of virgin harems? It seems to me that there should be as many religious philosophies as there are individuals who believe in a hereafter. It's *that* personal. The result of this religious individuation would be tinier ecumenical pissing matches (gushers to mere dribblings) over dogma or ecclesiastical differences, including whose fan club God loves best. Outright war between the masses could be replaced by, say, a game of checkers or a spelling bee between two individuals, or five rounds governed by the Marquis of Queensberry rules, or even pellet pistols at twenty paces, the worst case scenario being a world shortage of those black, elastic-banded eye patches that pirates wear. My position is that if everyone, including *you*, kept their afterlife beliefs private and personal—and, especially segregated from government—we'd all be the richer, the healthier, the wiser, the holier and happier for it aboard this glorious orb, God no-doubt the happiest of *all*. Amen.

You realize, of course, that readers, listeners, will cite you for blasphemy; however, since your poems seem to vacillate, leaning more toward the agnostic than atheistic, maybe you'll be granted forgiveness—perhaps readers taking the greatest umbrage will recognize hope yet for your salvation. You do care? You do struggle?

Daily. Make that hourly. Since you've read the poems, you know I was raised Catholic, something that nobody, in this brief history of time, has ever fully recovered from, and I don't necessarily mean this in a sarcastic vein, at least not entirely. Catholicism instilled a healthy dose of right-from-wrong during my upbringing, but no more so than did my dad, who showed little interest in the church. Augment a benevolent disposition with what I deem the Two Crucial Virtues, wisdom and forgiveness (or mercy) and that equips a person with all he or she needs to live life more as a *giver* than a *taker*. For the past decade, I've made the same new year's resolution, complete with my feel for poetic linebreak:

> Give and be giving
> And, especially, *be*
> Forgiving.

I fail miserably, more often than not, to adhere to this resolve, but I seldom lose my entire grip on the power of goodness which, again, I trace back to my virtuous upbringing, in the home more so than in the church. Catholicism, as is the case with most religions, is way too much about fear, and I am not willing to relinquish one of my four artistic *F*s, simple as that. *And....* (long, nervous pause)

For someone who boasts of fearlessness, why do you suddenly appear so skittish?

Earlier, you recall, I referenced "pedophile priests." (another pause) Somewhere in the closing pages of his memoir *Off To The Side*, Jim Harrison offers a quip about him and a friend being "short-funded" and regretting not having any "evil priests" in their boyhood past. It was hard not to chuckle, but it hit too close to home or, I should say, too close to St. Mary's Church back in 1963 or 1964. I was in seventh or eighth grade when the whisperings among us altar boys became all too loud. One friend, a lanky, tough Polish kid, was rumored to have hurdled the altar rail like Edwin Moses, yes *Moses*, during a dead-of-winter 6:00 a.m. mass, attended usually by a handful of old Italian women buried so deep in prayer that none would've noticed a frantic sprinter flashing by down the center aisle and busting out through the half-ton doors at the entrance to the church. It later became a matter of fact that the class nerd—defined here as the most innocent and submissive and, thus, most victimized—whose face I can clearly picture, and whose name I'll withhold, had been fondled on a table in the sacristy. Then one morning the predator priest singled me out as his prey at 5:30 a.m. as I was about to don my altar boy cassock. The guy was a heavyweight—had to be packing 250. Grabbed hold of me and was eager to show me, in his words, "the proper way to tuck your shirt into your trousers." Just as he was about to accomplish his demonstration, another priest walked in, quite unexpectedly. I remember the look on his face—he knew. The next morning, I showed up to serve mass with my dad's bone-handled hunting knife in my boot. I had watched too many westerns. I situated my bicycle, pointed downhill, at the bottom of the rectory stairs—imagining a cowboy making a fast break for his horse, ground-tied outside of a bank or saloon rather than a church. I had visualized sticking the priest then grabbing hold of my right, knife-wielding wrist with my left hand and leveraging a profound and literal upper-cut which would leave the bad guy down on bended knees and cradling his haggis sack in both forearms while I made my heroic escape unscathed. How goddamn *sad* is this all-too-true story? I weighed maybe 130 pounds. He trumped me double. I'll never forget the helplessness I felt in those powerful arms—will remember always my determination *not* to become preyed upon again, at whatever cost. I'll keep him anonymous, but I wonder if, in examining the church records, we'd find a certain priest listed as having been transferred suddenly to another parish during the early 1960s. He did not, I think it goes without saying, make a play for me that fateful, or faithful, morning. I remember my dad asking a day or so later if Father so-'n'-so had "monkeyed around"—is how he would've put it—with me or any of the other altar boys. I said "no." That evening I overheard him talking on the phone to his beer-drinking buddy, the other parish priest, who showed up in the nick of time that morning of the initial contact. Dad said something about "that goddamn queer" being gone by daybreak, "or else...." Never saw him again. Would I have stuck him? Saint Guido "The Fish" Muffasanti only knows. Did I feel I had the Good Lord's blessing to tack a proviso onto His commandment number five—"Thou shalt not kill," *unless* sexually molested by My clergy? Clearly I did. I wonder if this encounter with a so-called "man of the cloth" so-called "created in God's image" has more than a little to do with my absolute belief that no-frigging-way does *my* Creator sport a gender *or* a beard? On an even more caustic note, according to what I was taught in catechism, my beautiful father, as punishment for his non-church-going life, is, as we speak, suffering, burning, for eternity. I *dare* anyone to approach me with that contention regarding my dad's afterlife fate. I'll prove emphatically the difference between a peace advocate and a pacifist, the latter of which I am most definitely *not*. To close, I wrote a song lyric titled "God and Fear." It was in response to an onslaught of Rapture nonsense in the news— triggered by that series of Left Behind science-fiction books those two snake-oil-salesmen posing as legitimate authors were peddling by the millions. I actually, deep down, hope they're right. I hope the end of days *does* occur, the sooner the better. I would wring my hands in sheer devilment, as I happened upon a late model Dodge Ram diesel pickup idling—fuel tanks full— with the beamed-up former owner's empty duds crumpled in the driver's seat beneath a custom-made 100-X-beaver cowboy hat precisely my size, preferably black. Talk about "make *my* day." Back to "God and Fear," however. I'll recite only the choruses, which speak succinctly to my Christianity stance, and which also offer one of the most potent lyrical lines I've written:

Me and Jesus in a pickup
Going fishing, drinking beer
Cruising through The Masterpiece
Without guilt and without fear.

So me and Jesus, we go fishing
Talking creativity
"Praise Forgiveness!" is his mantra
"Renounce fear!" his decree.

Then me and Jesus, we go swimming
He's a fan of body art
BEING SCARED AIN'T BEING SACRED
Is tattooed above his heart.

That penultimate line?

Good ear.

So good, no way could I have missed the allusion to Stephen Hawking when you said, and I quote you verbatim, "Nobody, in this Brief History Of Time *has ever fully recovered from...."— in reference to having been raised Catholic. Stephen Hawking? You've read him?*

Tried to read him—after seeing him interviewed on *60 Minutes*. I don't remember the exact question the interviewer asked, but it addressed the motivational force behind Mr. Hawking's journeys deep into the mysteries of the universe. I'll never forget his response: "If we could discover why we and the universe exist, it would be the ultimate triumph of human reason—for then we would know the mind of God." It gives me chills to hear this aloud, although I have heard rumors that Stephen Hawking's forthcoming "M Theory" book offers far less theological manifestations. In any case, I watched, and listened to, this man field questions about his work and I could oh-so-humbly not help but compare his creative journeys into the unknown to those of the artist, and thus I have praised him often as the quintessential poet of our time. A piece that speaks facetiously to his prowess, "What Stephen Hawking, the Definitive Poet of All Time, Might, If He's Not Careful, Come Face-To-Surprising-Face With," is recorded, augmented with outrageous sound effects, on *Collisions of Reckless Love*. The pair of epigraphs we included are certainly far more profound than the poem. The first, by Albert Einstein, is well-documented: "Only two things are infinite—the Universe and human stupidity. And I'm not sure about the Universe." The second is from Montana Congresswoman—the very first woman elected to congress—Jeannette Rankin, who lived from 1880 to 1973. She was the only member of congress to vote against both WWI and WWII and, I believe, cast the sole dissenting vote for the latter. During her waning years she directed her anti-war sentiments toward Viet Nam. The epigraph by Ms. Rankin reads, "You can no more win a war than you can win an earthquake."

After hearing that marathon of a title and the pair of incredible epigraphs, how can we not ask to hear the poem as well?

Planet earth is the number one
rated, syndicated half-hour sitcom
showing on Universal Big Screen
Satellite TV. We have become such
natural born comedians, in fact,
that we've, in a mere century, outgrown
our need for the canned-laugh
soundtrack machine. Across the cosmos
intelligent life religiously watches us,
never missing an episode
because a good guffaw or, better yet,
belly laugh—they've known this
ever since something touched
off the mother of all fireworks
extravaganzas—is the only law, rule,
cure, hope, virtue, truth. When someone dies
they join the viewing audience
so fast, they host the hi-jinks
of their own wake, thus upping
one notch The Sagan Ratings. *Love?*

you ask. *Pain? Happiness? Loss? Despair?*
Courage, mercy, faith? Knee-slapping,
side-splitters all, yet not as slapstick hysterical
as our quest for success, security, status,
concepts so inane, they make black holes
look tangible as frothing pintfuls
of Guinness. There *is* great news,
however, tagged to this revelation
should it leave you distraught. Our world
will never end. We'll be forever
the longest running series
on The Eternity Network. We've become a cult hit
attracting *BILLions and BILLions* of devoted
viewers who believe
even our reruns are a riot.

For St. Claire—The Patron Saint of Television

*You have an undergraduate double major in biology and English,
so I suppose I shouldn't be surprised by the fine line you're sug-
gesting between the sciences and the arts.*

One more quote on that point, if I can find it here in one of
these notebooks. Here it is—from *Esquire* magazine, the August
2001 issue, an article titled *A Journey to the Beginning of Time*.
One Charles P. Pierce put it so eloquently when he said, "Our
place in the universe—where we place ourselves and why and
by whose grace, if by anybody's—always has been defined as
much by the art of imagination as by the calibrations of physical
science."

*Lovely. Anything else you want to add to our discussion of Poetry,
Religion, and the Art of Astrophysics?*

Only that someday soon I hope to take a shot at two poems,
the first—with which I've dabbled somewhat already—titled,
"Saint Peter Greets the Atheist Inside the Pearly Gates," and the
second, just a gleam in my ear thus far, triggered by Saint Francis
of Assisi.

I notice the New Mexico tinwork-framed magnetic image of him you have attached to the side of your Smith-Corona. Ever think of approaching Antiques Road Show for an appraisal of your typewriter?

Who was it that said, "There's a comedian in every interview?" You bet, "magnetic." This baby's made out of "good ol' U.S. of A. / steel and iron, truer than a shoeing anvil" to quote a passage from my poem "Why *I* Am Not Going to Buy a Computer," a title filched from a Wendell Berry essay. Once a year or so I stack the books I've published, along with my spoken-word CDs, as well as a couple of the songwriter disks on which my lyrics play a major role, and I lift the entire precarious tower off the desk. Here—try it. Come on—*try it*! Feel good? Go ahead—do a few curls. Calculate, calibrate, the weight of each critically-placed word—all those article and prepositional ounces, those hundreds of pounds of nouns, the action verb tonnage. Eat your heart out Arnie Schwarzenegger. When was the last time you literally held someone's life in your hands?

I have to ask: Do you know your fellow zed-man's, Warren Zevon's, poignant song, "Carmelita"? Its lyric strikes a degree of total despair that perhaps few songs have ever struck. The verse which....

> (Singing) "Well I pawned my Smith-Corona
> And I went down to meet my man
> He hangs out on Alvarado Street
> By the Pioneer Chicken stand.
> Carmelita, hold me tighter
> I think I'm sinking down
> I'm all strung out on heroin
> On the outskirts of town."

I don't care what Tom Russell says—you can sing when the pathos affects you this deeply. Or, at least—like your friend, Johnny Jasmann—you now and then "stumble onto the key of C."

Probably the latter. Russell actually recorded "Carmelita." So did Cross Canadian Ragweed, on *Happiness And All Other Things*, their CD I referenced earlier. And I agree with you about the song's despairing sentiment—it doesn't get any sadder on this planet than winding up so down and out, one is forced to pawn one's Smith-Corona.

Let's finally—before our capacity for earnestness runs thin—talk animals. Wildlife?

Liz and I spent Christmas 2009 in Santa Fe. We attended, with great humility, the Animal Dance on Christmas eve at Nambe Pueblo and the Turtle Dance at San Juan Pueblo the following afternoon. I skipped mass as I have done now for the past twenty or more Christmases, but I've never felt closer to some kind of sanctity as I did witnessing the Nambe dancers, in full animal horn and hide, as well as plant (gourd rattle, pine bow, etc.) regalia appear up out of the top of the kiva. Elk, antelope, bighorn sheep, buffalo, and deer dancers all moving together to the haunting drumbeat, to this earth's most organic, natural rhythms. Around and between the blazing *farolitos* and into the church—to bless *it*, Liz tells me, rather than to receive *its* blessing. During the Turtle Dance at San Juan, under what felt like the brightness of a July sun, the elders in their colorful wool blankets—the *caciques* overseeing the one-hundred-plus dancers—suddenly peered upward. We all, dancers included, followed their lead, and were graced by the sight of four eagles, three bald and one golden, circling high overhead. Big medicine, indeed. Most of the pueblo peoples being Christians, I don't think they'd mind me suggesting that Saint Francis of Assisi sent his messengers to approve. The coda to the dance might sound oddly concocted, but after returning to Montana we watched the film *Avatar*. Two-and-a-half hours later, we stepped out of the theater into yet one more otherworldly atmosphere, a heavy blizzard, which, lucky us, tempered what otherwise would've proved a rude re-entry. I drove us home into the blustery rural landscape, my face all but pressed against the windshield—jackrabbits, mule deer, and one magical, great horned owl swooping through the headlights. Thank you Saint Francis of Assisi *and* Richard Hugo for another opportunity to be "lost / in miles of land without people, without / one fear of being found...."

Saint Francis of Assisi—correct me if I'm wrong—is the patron saint of animals? And it's no secret that you've been writing more and more in celebration of their lives, their integral place in, and contribution to, "the glorious commotion of it all."

Or the glorious *communion* of it all. I can't imagine the planet, or poetry, without their presence. Or, as I wrote in the foreword to photographer Jay Dusard's *Open Country*: "Without wildlife, there is no musical score to this flick we call *Life on Earth*; without wildlife, the player piano has no holes in its roll." Do our animal brethren have souls? You goddamn right they do! Should they have rights, therefore, as well? I say, no question they should. Which is why I am a card-carrying member of the Montana Wilderness Association, the American Prairie Foundation, the World Wildlife Fund, the Natural Resources Defense Council, Defenders of Wildlife, *and* the Western Folklife Center in Elko. The latter should absolutely lengthen their handle to the *Wild* Western Folklife Center. That's the key word—WILD. "KEEP IT WILD!" to shout the Montana Wilderness Association's motto, a bumper-sticker I have glued to my black binder of works-in-progress. And speaking of religion again, in the *Good Book According to Zarzyski* (I've taken Emerson's advice, "Make your own bible."), the cowboy alongside the Indian tops the list of western wildlife. Also this proclamation, as long as my blood is quickly frothing to a brisk boil: No wide open spaces, no wild places, no need for the horse; no need for the horse, no need for the cowboy and, therefore, *no* way to separate wide open wild spaces from its wild diversity of wild constituents. Woven complexly into all of this fabric, of course, is the carnivorous make up of (I think?) the majority of species in the animal kingdom. I pretty much hung up my guns years ago—at around age 51, actually—after avidly hunting for over four decades of my life. I still eat meat, albeit less and less, but I see no reason to belittle or begrudge or be threatened by those who choose not to. A few years back at the Cowboy Poetry Gathering a middle-aged man from outside the ranching culture confided to me with a whisper that he was a vegetarian—that he "didn't want another living being to die in order for him to live." I'm not sure that's even possible. But I told him I admired his stance and considered it a "high calling." Those who want to eliminate every species that in any way threatens the financial gain of their occupation on the land are *not* venerators of the West—they're not *givers*, they're *takers*; they're not patrons and / or stewards, they're blasphemers and spoilers, tyrants and, far worse, tamers. "KEEP *IT* WILD!" That all-encompassing pronoun *IT*! Keep the land wild, keep the legacy wild, keep the life wild, keep the cowboy wild, keep the poetry wild, keep the heart wild, keep "the glorious communion-'n'-commotion of *IT* all" WILD! Which would be impossible without our fellow beings, our soulful poetic messengers, our kinfolk, by God!

You're shaking.

Are you a believer in Spontaneous Polish-Mafioso-Rodeo-Poet combustion? *Not* a pretty sight—or smell, for that matter.

Or not to mention the appearance of—and I quote you here— "the fucking mushroom cloud?"

You're very funny. I just hope my mother doesn't see this. She'd clap her prayerful hands, fingertips steepling toward heaven, beg forgiveness on our behalf for using the F-bomb in print, then proclaim her northern-Italian lament, *"El Mondo le Roto!"*

The world is broken?

You got *that* right.

With such mournful observation from the summit of Mount Zarzyski, let's begin what could become a lengthy difficult descent. You've commented somewhere—maybe in this very interview— that dozens of co-authors should accompany your name on the front cover of every book you've published. The intimation again is clear. "You get by with a little help from your friends." So... what about publishing?

I'm the world's biggest fan of creative collaboration. Never orchestrated a book that did not fit that description or definition. I absolutely adore the process. I've been extremely fortunate to have reveled in more than my share of these collaborations with publishers, editors, painters, photographers, playwrights, dance choreographers, musicians—my maestro amigos, producers Jim Rooney and Gordon Stevens, who've shared with me their recording studio passions, where the creative ethers levitated and elated me to some of my highest spiritual highs. Without a doubt, the recording studio is my poetry muse's five-star tryst hotel room of choice. To name a few other co-creators, Larry Pirnie—ahh, the magical times and projects we've celebrated together—Keith Browning, Barbara Van Cleve, Walter Piehl, Jim McCormick, Bob Blesse, Anne Widmark, Sue Rosoff, Kent Reeves, Jay Dusard, Paul Zimmer, Kathy Ogren, Mary Wachs, Mike Koppa, Emily Strayer, John Dofflemyer, Lance Belville, Lynn Lohr, Ted Waddell, Mike Hollern, Quinton Duval, Barbara and Ray March, who brought out *Wolf Tracks On The Welcome Mat*, and, now, Allen Jones of Bangtail Press, who promises to bring *51* into print, *if* he likes your interview. However, once the finished product—a book or CD or broadside—arrives and after we peruse those first copies out of the boxes, it mostly becomes an exercise in the anticlimactic. The only thing more difficult to market than a book or CD of poetry is arguably a book or CD of mime. I've boasted that my epitaph could read either, "He never left his publishers a penny in the red." Or the unfortunate flip side, "He never profited his publishers one red cent." My record producers are a sadder story altogether. For their sakes, I wish my name was Billy Collins.

You mentioned regretting not having co-written a song with Chris LeDoux. Reminiscent of the closing scene to Annick Smith's superb Richard Hugo documentary, Kicking The Loose Gravel Home—the scene in which Dick admits his litany of life's regrets—do you harbor a similar lengthy regrets list?

Did I mention that I've recently read Jim Harrison's memoir, *Off To The Side?* I bought an "uncorrected proof " copy in an odds-and-ends, secondhand shop in Fort Benton. My mom and dad were with me—here in town for the Montana Governor's Arts Award community celebration in April of 2005. I remember Dad delving into the book when we got back to the house and being absorbed by Harrison's stories—somewhat, I'll bet, because of Jim's interest in hunting and fishing, as well as his upbringing in Northern Michigan, that same Midwest landscape my dad embraced for almost eight decades at the time. Dad read a substantial portion of the book before flying back to Wisconsin. I didn't pick it up myself until recently. I *regret* not thinking to send the copy home with Dad so he could finish it. I'm amazed, in retrospect, that he related—an iron ore miner with a tenth grade education. Then again, he later worked for twenty years as Iron County's Drug and Alcohol Counselor—the subject of booze perhaps offering another plot of common ground in the memoir. So many chapters or episodes in Harrison's life feel foreign to *me*, not to mention that his exquisite prose is sometimes challenging. Also, not to mention how intimidated I am by the sheer numbers of books, of authors, he's read and readily references. Jim's a little older, but we grew up in the same neck of the woods, several hundred miles apart, in more or less the same era. But while he was reading the great works of literature I was watching westerns and biker flicks, football and boxing, on the Zenith. I *regret* how little I've read. *I regret* not taking Mom to Italy—by the time I was financially able, she said, "It's too late, they're all dead, what are we going to do, visit the cemeteries?" I *regret* not taking Dad on an Alaskan fishing trip. I *regret* not entering more rodeos, riding more bucking horses and spurring them prettier, hitting the big shows down south during the winter months. Had I been a more talented bronc rider, however, and thus been able to afford to spend more time on the circuit, I'd have written a lot fewer poems—which is to say, inherent in most regrets there exists thinly-disguised trade-offs. I *regret* not spending more time aboard good saddle horses—becoming an accomplished horseman. I *regret* every fellow being I've hunted and killed out of so-called "sport" rather than need. I *regret* not sticking with the guitar. I *regret* missing Woodstock. I *regret* a shitload of missed opportunities, as I'm guessing most people do—*regret* what I did not but could've done, rather than doing what I did but should not have done. I can still chip away at a few of the above regrets, but Dad's gone and Mom's pushing ninety. I'm very happy to say I have not a single regret about having helped my father exit this world with as much dignity as his medical situation allowed. I'm doing, and will continue to do, the same for Mom. No question, those two non-regrets offer an ultimate trump to the misfires I've just listed.

In Off To The Side, *Harrison devotes a chapter to each of what he calls his "Seven Obsessions," seven being his favorite number. Your number of choice—alongside the far too unwieldy 51—is eight. How would you declare and define your eight, shall we say, gravitations—things, activities, places, idealisms, passions, forces, etc., toward which you are attracted? Although "Eight Gravitations" does lack the organic ring of "Seven Obsessions," let's concede to Mr. Harrison, as preface to your* hommage?

Yes, let's do make that concession. And let's not, moreover, list Jim's seven. Well, maybe just a *tease*, without apologies for the pun, as one of Jim's obsessions is—are you ready for this— "stripping." Yes, ladies and gentlemen, even major literary figures dig a little ecdysiast T-'n'-A. My "Eight Gravitations" have been updated, I should admit. A decade or so ago they would've likely included "Hunting and Fishing," "Rodeo and Horses," and maybe "Back Road Montana Watering Holes." Here then are the eight holding fast thus far in the new millennium:

1. **Stuff**: A term that best-defines my prized possessions, collectibles, keepsakes, memorabilia, my *Forty Years Gatherings*, to quote the title of that stellar Spike Van Cleve book (Barbara's dad). I suppose I fancy myself the rodeo-cowboy-turned-antique-scout, the protagonist picker (finder of stuff), Jack McGriff, in the fine, early McMurtry novel, *Cadillac Jack*. None of the synonyms for "stuff" I listed above, however, compare with that most consoling euphemism, "material culture," which I first heard from my dear Elizabeth Dear, a museum curator and folklorist. Yes sir, I'm a serious connoisseur and collector of material culture, a Polish-Eye-talian pack rat—I haul shit home. Just look around us here in this crammed little room. Moreover, quiz friends Larry Pirnie, Lyle Meeks, Mike Hollern, about helping me move across town, Christmas of 1996, forty below zero. Ask Ralph Beer about dead-lifting my box of "unusual rocks," then wrestling it up out of the basement of his Missoula house I once rented and into the back of my pickup. The saddest event I actually admit looking forward to attending is an estate sale. Liz and I do not have children. Someday—hopefully not too soon—the picker-vultures will anticipate *our* estate sale with hand-wringing revel.

2. **Unusual Food and Barley Soup**: I boasted earlier that I've never been a finicky eater, but I have become a lot fussier about the beer I drink. Back in the grad school day, a 99 cent sixer of Lucky or Buckhorn more than filled the bill. Prior to that, as sixteen-year-olds packing fake I.D.s in Hurley, we'd spill our pocket change on the bar at Pete's Tavern and hope its total

was dime-devisable by two—$3.60 meant eighteen 10 cent taps apiece, likely Schlitz or Black Label. Today my taste in hops is a bit advanced from our 1960s anything-with-or-without-a-head brewski imbibing. And I especially love the stouts and the porters, all porters, as well as the word, "porter" itself, which, after quaffing several porters always looks more and more like the word "poeter," reason enough not to quit after just one or two, right? I like my beer, as I like my coffee, thick enough to float a sailor's upper plate, a shore leave whore's glass eye, or vice versa. (And you would've wagered I'd have said "float a horseshoe.") As for slightly more-solid nourishment, back when I filled a couple freezers with venison, elk, antelope, game birds, ducks, and, *just once*, mountain goat, I cooked daily and mostly excelled at the art of preparing game. Today I grow fonder and fonder of good restaurants, thanks mostly to the east and the *left* coasts I more often visit, as well as to Santa Fe where we make our biannual pilgrimages. And also where I came face-to-steaming-face—no thanks to Liz's brother, virtuoso silversmith David Dear—with the only food in decades that I could not, hard as I tried, wrap my palate around. *Si, mi amigo, menudo.*

A close second to this unsavory Mexican cuisine episode, involved the aforementioned mountain goat. Damn near died up on Bass Creek in the Bitterroots after swallowing a fistful of an equine anti-inflammatory drug to relieve the swelling in my throbbing knees. Woke up in a pup tent in the middle of the night, my entire body on fire, and figured I'd be a goner by dawn. Shot the goat, packed the meat, head, and cape out, put the tenderloins in a hot cast iron pan a day later, and watched them inflate into the rubber, tie-rod end bushings of a Ford half ton. My hunting partner, Steve Anders, having shot several goats over the decades, declined my offer to split the meat fifty-fifty, which I found odd, until I discovered that I couldn't scratch the surface of a chop with a diamond-toothed Husqvarna, and that my dog glowered in disgust at his bowl filled with fresh meat. A year or two later—purely out of guilt for having needlessly taken the life of this celestial, bearded being—I thawed every remaining package and concocted the mother of all mountain goat meat loafs. We're talking bacon, garlands of garlic, onions, celery, bell peppers, several handfuls of chili pequin, a bottle of Worcestershire, copious splashes of Tabasco, a half-gallon of screw-top Beaujolais, and an inch-thick smothering of doctored-up chipotle tomato paste over the top. I likely placed jugs of my dad's rock-'n'-rye moonshine and Johnny Alleva's grappa on the table, filled the extra refrigerator with my friends' favorite brand of cheap beer, and might've even rented a couple porn videos to further distract the dinner guests from the main course—all for naught. They drank every drop of spirits, cleaned up the chips and side dishes, barely touched the *piece de resistance* I'd worked so stealthily to prepare, and then they left, left me with no less than fifteen pounds of goat loaf, every bite of which I was determined, with or without the dog's help, to consume—again, out of guilt and stubbornness—even after it started to grow a greenish-pink punk hair-do two weeks later in the frig. You did not waste food in the 1950s and 1960s at 505 Poplar Street. My dad told story after story about what he and his twelve brothers and sisters had, and did not have, to eat during the Depression.

3. **The Boob Tube and Moviedom:** In the poem "Cowboys and Indians," I speak to the intimate childhood moments spent with my dad in front of the television set. I reference it also in the introduction to *Blue-Collar Light*. I relate how, after picking dew worms until 11:30 p.m. on a meatless, religious Friday, Dad and I would watch the late movie—usually *Run Silent, Run Deep* with Clark Gable—and how, seconds after midnight, Dad would serve super-sized portions of sirloin steak smothered in his garden onions and wild, stump mushrooms, which we had also picked together. We'd sop up the pink juices pooling on our platters with "Dago bread" *pietkas* (my dad called them *pimkas)*—the Polish word for the butt ends of the loaf. Picture tubes and silver screens played a much larger role in my blue-collar Midwest upbringing than did books, I am both sorry and not sorry to admit. For years, during Sunday afternoons I would lie on my belly on the living room floor, Dad in his threadbare, Archie Bunker chair behind me, watching Walter Cronkite's *The Twentieth Century*. Every week, I would secretly hope to see footage of British soldiers during World War II so I could *innocently* ask, again and again without Dad ever catching on—he was *that* ensconced in the program—"Dad, who are those guys in the funny helmets?" "Goddamn limey sons-a-bitches," he'd inform me, as I muffled the laughter into the crook of my arm and the shag carpet. Never did inquire as to the reason behind his harsh sentiment of our allies, but my best guess is that it had something to do with Field

Marshal Montgomery's exploits. To this day, if I find myself sinking, lump-throated, toward rock bottom and desperately in need of a chuckle to buoy me out of the doldrums, I relive those "goddamn limey sons-a-bitches" Sunday afternoons with Dad, which brings both smiles and tears to my face. I pray—yes, *pray*—however, that you'll forgive me this anecdote, my dear, *dear* friend, Peter O'Brien, of London.

4. **Blue-Collar Euphoria**: I tell the story about my dad, at seventy-nine or eighty, sitting in his chair and reading the *Ironwood Daily Globe* late one summer night, after putting in no less than a sixteen-hour day of chores that involved heavy physical labor. I was watching TV when he startlingly crumpled the paper down from over his face and into his lap and pronounced with intense urgency that we better get *this* and *this* and *this* done tomorrow. He lifted the *Globe* back up to continue reading. Hard as I tried to bite my lip, I replied, "*Why* at your age can't you relax—*why* do you find it necessary to work yourself to exhaustion day after day?" Without a second's hesitation, he lowered the newspaper far more gently this time to just below his chin—and enunciated his four-syllabled response as if it were the sacred password that would swing gloriously open the pearly gates: "Sat-is-fac-tion." The "-tion" just barely making it over the top of the newsprint as it rose back over his face. I can think of few conversations in my life that closed on such a sockdolager of a conclusive note.

My younger brother, Gary, has often accused me of being S.O.L.—no, not Shit-Outta-Luck, but Son-Of-Leonard. The poem, "How I Tell My Dad I Love Him," says it better than I can here, but, chip-off-the-ol'-blockski that I've become, I too am a fan of hard physical work. It's the "John Henry" syndrome, thank you very much Woody Guthrie and Tennessee Ernie Ford. I remember working—repaving Highway 51, in fact—for Gasser Construction Company, summer of 1969, earning money for my first year of college at Stevens Point. I was 180 pounds of "greased Eye-talian tank," to quote Burgess Meredith in *Rocky*. I watched as three men with a front-end loader chained up several ten-foot railroad ties and hoisted them onto a flatbed trailer. I knew I could do it faster without the machine, and set out to prove it. The company foreman practically begged me to stay on at the end of August. At age eleven I met Jack Miller, the first friend who owned a set of weights. We began lifting together and later played high school football for the Hurley Midgets—yes, the Midgets. Just received my March 2010 retirement account statement from Jack's Edward Jones office in Seattle. Here it is right here—see for yourself. "Total Account Value, $8,659.58." I am more than a little relieved to say I've stayed in pretty good shape over the decades and, like my dad, hope to be able to put in a full day of physical labor into my eighties—with an IRA like mine, you goddamn well *better* be able to, no?

5. **Fellow Beings**: We've discussed this beyond the saturation point already, but when it comes to our animal brethren, I've become more and more a sentimental mush-heart, to the degree that road-kill victims sadden me to the quick. Making our way toward Lewistown just east of the Snowy Mountains, returning from visiting Mom last November, I spotted a Great Pyrenees standing vigil on a knoll among a herd of sheep not too far off the shoulder-less two-lane. Within a second of proclaiming its majestic presence to Liz, who was driving, I caught a quick glimpse of its mate dead in the barrow pit. Shattered my heart into so many pieces I still—months later—haven't glued the shards back into place. I don't know why, or how, I take these moments so personally. Maybe I need professional help, but I'm resisting therapy for a good reason—the fewer possessives you claim at the end of your life, the bigger the prize, says I. So far there's merely *my* dentist, George, *my* barber, also George, *my* mechanics, Tim and Jim, *my* travel agent, Tracey, *my* publisher, Allen, and *my* friend, Jack, who manages *my* minuscule portfolio, but who I refuse to tag as *my* broker. Which is all to say, I am not willing to add *my* therapist, *my* "mind doctor," to the list—yet. I think you can understand, however—although I sure couldn't when watching my dad mothball his rifles and shotguns—my slow but steady aversion to hunting, which I lived for as a younger man. You know, the more I ponder this excessive sentimentality, the more I realize I've likely lived with it my entire life—thank you, Mother. She sang sentimental animal songs to me as an infant, in sentimental Italian, no less, and I don't think I've ever recovered:

Limos, limosette	Snail, little snail,
Pecha for chel belle ochlette	Peek out with your beautiful eye,
O' visin, o' lonton	Either near or far away
Ge serra el so compagne.	Your companion should come by.

I remember having pet rabbits, my overworked dad having to build more and more hutches until one day he informed me that I'd have to consider butchering and eating them. We devised a scheme. My uncle Albert owned a hardware store. We drew up a pool with twenty-five numbered squares which he posted near the cash register. "Win a large domestic rabbit"—to cook, was the supposition—"4 bits per chance." In a matter of days, the card was filled. We drew a number and the winner, Mr. Erspamer, happened to live a few houses away. It was dark, snowing heavily. I went out to the hutches and decided on a very large white female whose name, thank goodness, I can't recall (or otherwise I'd be blubbering—again). I walked up the street, taking six-inch steps, and knocked on elderly Mr. Erspamer's door with hopes he wouldn't be home. Hard to describe the surprise in his face when he saw me standing there with, I'm sure, glassy eyes and my arms wrapped tight around a twenty-pound, pink-eared main ingredient for hasenpfeffer. After telling him he'd won the pool, he replied, "I thought you'd deliver it butchered and ready for the stew pot. You keep it son. I don't want it." Not only did I get to put my cherished pet back into her hutch but I made $12.50. My dad just shook his head and laughed when I told him. It was one of the happiest moments of my life, and certainly indicative of just how pathetic a 4-H member I'd have been.

The older I get, the more desperately I seek out wisdom from intelligent fellow beings, albeit more difficult to discover beauty-and-truth virtues among my own species. If life on earth is a symphony, delivering what amounts to a single *note's worth* of orchestral contribution to the universe's ultimate, infinite composition, then we *need* to bring every single music-maker we can to this planet's stage. Furthermore, if divine evolution had gone somehow askew and resulted in a homophonic, homochromatic animal kingdom of solely Homo sapiens, then earth would have been reduced, in my view, to a *noteworthy-less* orb. (long silence)

6. **Friends and Letters**: Among my hoards of **Stuff** are dozens of antique leather and hard-cloth suitcases filled with correspondence going back forty years. Many of the letters are from Mom and Dad. A few are from erstwhile girlfriends, although after at least one breakup I recall burning a grocery sack full. Most are from folks who have befriended me, and I them, along the poetry trails. My compadre, Paul "Red" Shuttleworth,

is no doubt singlehandedly responsible for an entire suitcase. He's told me on numerous occasions how he hauls his accumulated correspondence regularly to the burn barrel—"to save us from the carcass fuckers," is how he crudely couches it. Although I understand his sentiments and have witnessed complete strangers reading shoeboxes of intimate letters found in estates, I find it difficult to even think about destroying my pickup truck load of correspondence. Another friend, Jim McLeod, who's also well-represented in the Zarzyski archives, recently informed me that he's actually spoken on my behalf with the University of Montana archivist who expressed interest in my "papers." All I know from this vantage point is that before *any* writer decides to place his or her correspondence into the public's trust, he or she should read the published letters of, say, Ernest Hemingway. Little could most of us ever fathom, decades later, the degree to which our intended personal and private scribblings could lean toward such pinnacles of sheer profanity, absolute unshackled rankness. These concerns aside, however, what has pestered me over the decades is how the correspondence has so often gotten between me and my extremely jealous, possessive Muse. Her exacted vengeance—when interaction with others was given priority over intercourse with Her—has brought me all too often to my knees and weeping at her scarlet-polished toenails, as I pleaded for that precise word or line She was depriving me of. With the advents of both e-mail and flat-rate telephone plans, I've been granted some relief from letter writing. Here's my current rubber-banded bundle. Let's count. Not bad—a mere twenty-three letters in arrears. Can hardly wait to finish this interview so I can begin catching up with these dear friends, first thing tomorrow morning.

7. **Solitude:** Chekov said, "True happiness is impossible without solitude. The fallen angel probably betrayed God because he longed for solitude, which angels do not know." Philippe Petit speaks to the savoring of solitude out on the wire. My dad, in an arc above the door of his "shack" on "the 20," christened his get-away abode, S E R E N I T Y, with well-spaced hardwood letters he fashioned on his band saw. He'd spent hundreds of nights there alone, almost every one of which included the scrawling of a south-pawed letter to me. Since his death, I have promised the stars I'd stay a night there at the oak table he built—writing poetry. Maybe this spring when the big trees begin donning their

summer crowns, begin drawing up into their canopy the spirit of Dad's remains I spread around their trunks last fall. I know the poems wait patiently for me there, and I *will* greet them. All to say, I guess I'm also s.o.l., "son of Leonard," when it comes to my need for solitude. How ironic it is, then, that performing poetry from the stage—the very antithesis to the solitude required in which to write the poems—has favored my life with some its most exhilarating moments. Highlights include an evening shared with legend Ian Tyson and the Reno Philharmonic Orchestra, conducted by maestro extraordinaire Barry Jekowsky, another with Wylie & The Wild West, conductor Eckart Preu and the Spokane Symphony, as well as stages shared with Garrison Keillor and Stephanie Davis, with Wally McRae, Tom Russell, Chris LeDoux, Greg Keeler, Rambling Jack Elliott, Horse Sense, Riders In The Sky, Cowboy Celtic, John Dofflemyer, Henry Real Bird, Buck Ramsey, and numerous, numerous other poets and musicians so adept at enchanting their audiences. Oh sure, there were those nights that made me beg on bended knee never again to have to step out from behind the curtain into the lights. Like the time they pulled the plug on my mike after just three poems at a Freemont Street venue in Vegas—pulled it to literally save me from incurring artistic self-annihilation as my words were falling light years shy of the intoxicated audience's ears. It took years to recover from the humiliation. Today, finally, I can admit out loud my failure at that Vegas event, complemented with the orgulous boast, "How many *other* performers do you know who've been paid a G-note per poem, *plus* come away from the gig with photographs of themselves book-ended by drop-dead gorgeous, scantly feather-clad showgirls?" Despite crash-'n'-burns such as this, I continue to book gigs—thanks to my one-n-only agent friend ever, Sande DeSalles—to show up, and to do my best to deliver the goods. It's gotten beyond difficult, however, to leave the page behind in exchange for the stage. In no small part *because* I find myself—the older I get and the longer I write—garnering more and more "sat-is-fac-tion," as well as validation, from the page. And the older I get, the more desperate I become to stake out the time I'll need, and then some, to write the thousands of poems beckoning me to bring them to the page before I cash in the proverbial ol' chiparooskis. I hope I don't sound like an ingrate, especially to those who've applauded, celebrated, supported my work over the years. I feel eternally indebted. It's been a privilege to make my living as a performance poet. And yet I remain steadfast in my pursuit of solitude. No solitude, no page—no page, *no* stage.

I wasn't going to offer a single interjection during your Eight Gravitations, but isn't the opposite or reverse also somewhat true—no stage, no page?

To a degree, you're absolutely right, *if* we are talking "published page." In my case, 95 percent of the books I've placed, I've placed because of my profile on the stage. I'd hate to even consider how few we'd have sold—incognito, so to speak—off the bookstore shelves. You make a strong point, damn you, but now back to the gravitation at hand, **Solitude.**

In the 1950s, as a young boy growing up in Hurley, I knew a number of folks referred to, by grownups and children alike, as "retarded." One of these people, Gingy Wallis, lived just down the block from us. Last November when I was back in Hurley to celebrate Mom's eighty-ninth birthday, I discovered that Gingy's given name was Donald Wallis. Beautiful ring—Donald Wallis. He had a thick mustache and big wild hair. He smoked cigars, talked to himself—which, obviously, in light of this self-interview, no longer alarms me—and often appeared agitated or angry. In retrospect, I'd have been rattled too had I been the victim of all the teasing, taunting, and mocking I saw inflicted upon him. I was five or six years old, and Gingy frightened me. One day, while I was sitting on the stoop in front of our house, along he comes with his border collie-mongrel-cross on a tight leash. When the dog lunged at me playfully for a pet and I reached out, Gingy yanked it away and growled, "Doan bodder me—doan bodder me bar dawggies needer." Don't bother me and don't bother my dog, either. I was too startled to move. He stood there smoking his stogie and gawking in any direction that left me out of his sight. I swallowed hard, worked up some courage, and asked, "Where you been, Gingy? I haven't seen you for a long time." "Been to the farn-*ay*, been to the farn-*ay*," he replied. "Oh, the *farm*," I said. "Any animals on the farm?" "God-dan right, dey got an'mals on da farn-*ay*. Got moon-*ay* cow, big moon-*ay* cow, liddo moon-*ay* cow. Got horse-*ay*, chick-*ay*, big chick-*ay*, liddo chick-*ay*, turk-*ay*, got turk-*ay*, big turk-*ay*, liddo turk-*ay*...." I've told this story in private over the years to friends who I knew in advance had been cursed with the same warped sense of humor as mine. It doesn't seem anywhere near as lighthearted now, however, as I wonder if Gingy had actually been to an agricultural farm or rather to what folks in his presence likely referred to as *the* farm, as in "funny farm." I wonder also if "Old McDonald had a farm" had been sung to him as a child, thus his familiar litany of the animals. To finish the story, I sadly succumbed that day—likely out of some misconstrued rite of passage—to a form of vexation I'd observed from older kids and adults unafraid of Gingy. "Any giraffes on the farm, Gingy?" I prodded. "God-dan right, dey got g'raff-*ays* on da farn-*ay*—big g'raff-*ays*, liddo g'raff-*ays*—god-dan right dey got g'raff-*ays*...."

Fifty-five years later, I'll be sitting here, early morning, in this little writing sanctuary, swallowed up in the solitude of my voluptuous Muse's arms—my mascot Zeke-the-blue-eyed-Aussie sprawled asleep alongside my chair—when the phone I forgot to take off the hook blasts all three of us back to miasmic reality. Cringing, I look down at Zeke peering anxiously up at me in anticipation of the response he's come to expect: "Doan bodder me—doan bodder me bar dawggies, needer," I enunciate slowly, laughing as his ears perk to that familiar word in his lexicon, "dawggies." I've read a little of the touted philosophers—Plato, Nietzsche, Jung, etc.—but none of their words of wisdom hold sway and ring more profoundly than, in light of my current quest for solitude, the words of Doctor of Philosophy Professor, Donald Wallis: "Don't bother me, and don't bother my dog, either."

8. **Private Piety, Personal Eternity**: I'd be wise to exercise my earlier exhortation, keep what I intend to say here to myself, and maybe even leave this final gravitation completely blank. In the words of one of my favorite troupes of cowboy musicians, Riders In The Sky, "That would be the easy way, but it wouldn't be the *cowboy* way!" The practice of spirituality or spiritualism, for me, has mostly to do, let me repeat, with the enlightened pursuit and acquisition of wisdom, which is buoyed by truth. I recently bought a bumper sticker—in the Salt Lake City airport, of all places—that reads, "Militant Agnostic: I Don't Know And You Don't Know Either." Agnosticism, however, doesn't define my stance, which, if pressed, I'd say is a cross between pantheism and deism—Pandeism. Anthropologist Joseph Campbell, in his lectures titled, "The Shaping of Our Mythic Traditions," quotes

a twelfth century piece of writing: "God is an intelligible sphere whose center is everywhere and circumference nowhere." As I intimated earlier, I believe in an ego-less Supreme Maker, so open-hearted, so infused with creative spirit, it is *expected* of us to question the Artistic Vision, the Workings, the Masterpiece. The Supreme Maker I believe in does not want to be feared, is *not* punitive, does not play favorites, and is repulsed, as am I, by that pretentious declaration, "There, but for the grace of God, go I." The Creator I place my faith in also loathes both ethnocentrism and anthropocentrism. Lest you forget, however, I am *not* seeking converts. Not only do I not expect anyone to agree *ad litteram* with this doctrine, with my individual tenets, I actually hope no one does, as there's merely room enough for one, maybe two, in my personal church. In closing, the molested altar boy I referenced earlier is named David. Saint David is the patron saint of poets and writers. Translated in Hebrew, David means "beloved." I hope he's well. I hope he's slain his Goliath demons, and is healing and living up to his name.

Now I'm the one who's shaking. I'm the one in need of an emotional emollient. Humor me for a moment, please. I just realized that considering the length of this interview it's doubtful there'll be room for photographs. For those readers who do not know you, haven't seen you, how about a brief description?

Sure. I'm a cross between a youthful Richard Boone in his role as Paladin, Sam Elliott, Leonardo DiCaprio, Mozart, and Edgar Allan Poe, only with a lot more hair—most of it, unfortunately, on my brisket.

Thanks. Let's wrap this up. The flipside of regrets is, perhaps, remaining aspirations. What's left—where to from here?

Have you seen the film *Crossroads?*

I have.

Why am I not surprised. Then you remember the old blues musician, Willy Brown, played by that virtuoso of an actor, Joe Seneca—what an absolutely beautiful face! He's partnered-up with the young protégé, played by Ralph Macchio of *The Karate*

Kid fame. They bust Willy Brown out of the nursing home and make a pilgrimage to a deep-south crossroads where Willy, in his foolish youth, made a pact, a contract, with the Devil, and is hoping to void it. I can't help but to interject a couple of marvelous passages that surface in the film. Old Willy saying, "Blues ain't nothing but a good man feelin' bad, thinking' about the woman he was once with." Or this gem, "Robert Johnson gave us twenty-nine songs and that's enough." Anyway, they cross paths again with old Beelzebub, who pitches them a deal. If Willy's young guitar ace will "cut heads" with the devil's ace and out-duel him, then Lucifer will rip up the contract. Macchio, trained at Julliard, throws the knockout punch with a riff that includes a myriad of classical notes that the devil's man, portrayed by rock guitarist Steve Vai, cannot respond to, cannot trump. The contract is ripped in two, and Willy and his boy are beamed back to the gravel crossroads. "I hear Chicago callin'," Willy delights. "You ready for The Windy City?" But then he announces, to the boy's chagrin, "After Chicago, you on your own." When Macchio protests and asks "*Why?*" Willy replies, "Cuz you got to take the music someplace else—take it past where you found it. That's what *we* did."

Thusly, for me, that's what it *has* to be all about—taking the music, taking the poetry, past where I found it. I could care less, please understand, about overcoming some *poète maudit* complex. Rather, because my development's been slow, I'll simply need to inhabit this planet awhile longer. So I'm swallowing vitamins and supplements by the fistful. I'm doing my sit-ups, my push-ups, my A.A.R.P. (Ain't Able to Remember Poop) rounds on the heavy bag. I've been writing poetry for almost forty years and another couple-three decades would maybe enable me to ratchet or leverage "my craft or sullen art" a notch or two beyond where I discovered it. If I can accomplish this, perhaps I'll be deserving—before some major big-ring poetry show—of the literary world's version of boxing's memorial ten-count tolling of the bell. I can't ask for anything more than that, can I? Except, to be on the receiving end of Mexican Artist Frieda Kahlo's sentiment: "I hope the exit is joyful and I hope never to return."

To be continued?

245

ACKNOWLEDGMENTS

The author and publisher are grateful to the editors of the following journals, magazines, and anthologies, in which a number of the poems from this collection first appeared, many in earlier drafts: *Suisun Valley Review, The Chariton Review, Talking River Review, Viceroy, Modoc Independents News, Poemeleon: A Journal of Poetry, Mo: Writings from the River, Sweet Nothings: An Anthology of Rock and Roll in American Poetry, Spit In the Ocean #7: All About Kesey, Open Range: Poetry of the Reimagined West, Poems Across the Big Sky: An Anthology of Montana Poets,* and *New Poets of the American West.*

Our gratitude, as well, to producers, Jim Rooney of Jim Rooney Productions, and Gordon Stevens, Tim Volpicella, Lee Ray, and Scott Sorkin of Open Path Music for recording numerous poems and lyrics included in *51,* on the following four spoken-word CDs: *Words Growing Wild* and *The Glorious Commotion of it All* (JRP); *Rock 'n' Rowel* and *Collisions of Reckless Love* (OPM).

Some of the poetry woven into the Self-Interview was formerly published in *Wolf Tracks on the Welcome Mat* (Oreanabooks, 2003), *Blue-Collar Light* (Red Wing Press, 1998), *All This Way for the Short Ride* (Museum of New Mexico Press, 1996), *I Am Not A Cowboy* (Dry Crik Press, 1995), and *The Garnet Moon* (The Black Rock Press, 1990). Thank you to the publishers and editors of these volumes for their permission to reprint the work.

Finally, our very gracious tip-of-the-hat appreciation to the singer-songwriter artist friends and their record companies for including the following lyrics on their albums (chronologically according to the CD release date):

"Maria Benitez" (John Hollis—*Good Life,* Skookum Music, 2000)

"Black Upon Tan" (David Wilkie, Denise Withnell, and Cowboy Celtic—*The Drover Road,* Centerfire Music / Shanachie /

Western Jubilee Recording Co., 2001)

"Jerry Ambler" (Ian Tyson—*Ian Tyson, Live At Longview*, Slick Fork Music / Vanguard Records, 2002)

"All This Way for the Short Ride" and "Bucking Horse Moon" (Tom Russell— *Indians Cowboys Horses Dogs*, Frontera Music / Hightone Records, 2004)

"Hope Chest," "Lucky Charms of Love," "The Christmas Saguaro Soiree," and "The Best Dance" (Betsy Hagar—*Heavens to Betsy*, Side B Music, 2004)

"A Pony Called Love," "Double Wild," "Hang-n-Rattle!" (Wylie Gustafson—*Hang-n-Rattle!*, Two Medicine Music, 2009)

"Maestro" and "Wicked Kiss" (Wylie Gustafson—*Raven On The Wind*, Two Medicine Music, 2011)

"Flyin', Not Fallin', in Love with You" (David Wilkie, Denise Withnell—*Rose Petal Pie*, Centerfire Music, 2011)

Special thanks to producer John Carter Cash for the inspiration behind the inclusion of "Bob Dylan Bronc Song" as a spoken-word hidden track on *Hang-'n'-Rattle!*

This book would never have come to fruition without the friendship, encouragement, and keen sensibilities of Elizabeth Dear, Quinton Duval, Gary Thompson, Anne Widmark, Sally Phelan, Sue Lyons, Gordon and Judith Stevens, Kathy Ogren, Wylie Gustafson, Zeke Zarzyski, and Allen Jones.

Photo by Kevin Martini-Fuller

ABOUT THE AUTHOR

Paul Zarzyski, a 1951 model, hails from 505 Poplar Street in Hurley, Wisconsin— "Where (highway) 51 ends and the Fun Begins." The wellsprings of his writing pour forth from a rich poetic lineage composed of the north woods fishing, hunting, mushroom-picking, firewood-making appetites of his dad, Leonard, and the Italian kitchens steeped in old-country cooking graced with the soulful lilts of his mother, Delia.

Under the tutelage of poet Richard Hugo, Paul received his M.F.A. degree in 1976 from the University of Montana, where he later taught, while also competing as a rodeo circuit bareback bronc rider. This year, 2011, marks his twenty-fifth consecutive annual *go-'round* at the National Cowboy Poetry Gathering in Elko, Nevada—the humbling good fortune which Paul credits as the driving force behind his poetic voice in the West, which, in turn, has favored his work with venues such as the Library of Congress, the Kennedy Center Millennium Stage, Festival Hall in London, and Garrison Keillor's *A Prairie Home Companion*.

The author of eight books and four spoken-word CDs, Paul currently is learning to apply his poetics to the art of the lyric, and has co-written songs with eminent mentors Ian Tyson, Tom Russell, David Wilkie, Betsy Hargar, and Wylie Gustafson, the latter with whom he shared a 2010 Spur Award from the Western Writers of America for Best Western Song ("Hang-n-Rattle!"). He also received the 2010 Spur Award for his poem "Bob Dylan Bronc Song," and the 2004 Spur for his poetry collection, *Wolf Tracks on the Welcome Mat*, as well as the 1996 Western Heritage Wrangler Award from the National Cowboy Hall of Fame for his book, *All This Way for the Short Ride*. Honoring his life's work, the Montana Governor's Arts Award for Literature was presented to Paul for 2005.

Paul currently lives west of Great Falls with arts historian and C. M. Russell scholar Elizabeth Dear, their Aussie dog, Zeke, and horses, Pecos and Lash.

CPSIA information can be obtained at www.ICGtesting.com
Printed in the USA
BVOW031251140612

292097BV00008B/2/P